Take It to Your Seat Centers Math 6

Using the Centers

The 12 centers in this book provide hands-on practice to help students master standards-based mathematics skills. It is important to teach each skill and to model the use of each center before asking students to do the tasks independently. The centers are self-contained and portable. Students can work at a desk, at a table, or on a rug, and they can use the centers as often as needed.

Why Use Centers?

- Centers are a motivating way for students to practice important skills.
- They provide for differentiated instruction.
- They appeal especially to kinesthetic and visual learners.
- They are ready to use whenever instruction or practice in the target skill is indicated.

Before Using Centers

You and your students will enjoy using centers more if you think through logistical considerations. Here are a few questions to resolve ahead of time:

- Will students select a center, or will you assign the centers and use them as a skill assessment tool?
- Will there be a specific block of time for centers, or will the centers be used by students throughout the day as they complete other work?
- Where will you place the centers for easy access by students?
- What procedure will students use when they need help with the center tasks?
- Will students use the answer key to check their own work?
- How will you use the center checklist to track completion of the centers?

Introducing the Centers

Use the teacher instructions page and the student directions on the center's cover page to teach or review the skill. Show students the pieces of the center and model how to use them as you read each step of the directions.

If you find some of the skills too challenging for your students, you may want to use one or more of the centers only for group work, or you might use the center several times with a group before assigning it for independent use. You also have the option of assigning only part of a center for independent work.

Recording Progress

Use the center checklist (page 4) to record both the date when a student completes each center and the student's skill level at that point.

Making the Centers

Included for Each Center

Ⓐ Student directions/cover page

Ⓑ Task cards and mats

Ⓒ Reproducible activity

Ⓓ Answer key

Materials Needed

- Folders with inside pockets
- Small envelopes or self-closing plastic bags (for storing task cards)
- Pencils or marking pens (for labeling envelopes)
- Scissors
- Double-sided tape (for attaching the cover page to the front of the folder)
- Laminating equipment

How to Assemble and Store

1. Tape the center's cover page to the front of the folder.
2. Place reproduced activity pages and a supply of scratch paper in the left-hand pocket of the folder.
3. Laminate mats and task cards.
4. Cut apart the task cards and put them in a labeled envelope or self-closing plastic bag. Place the mats and task cards in the right-hand pocket of the folder. If you want the centers to be self-checking, include the answer key in the folder.
5. Store prepared centers in a file box or a crate.

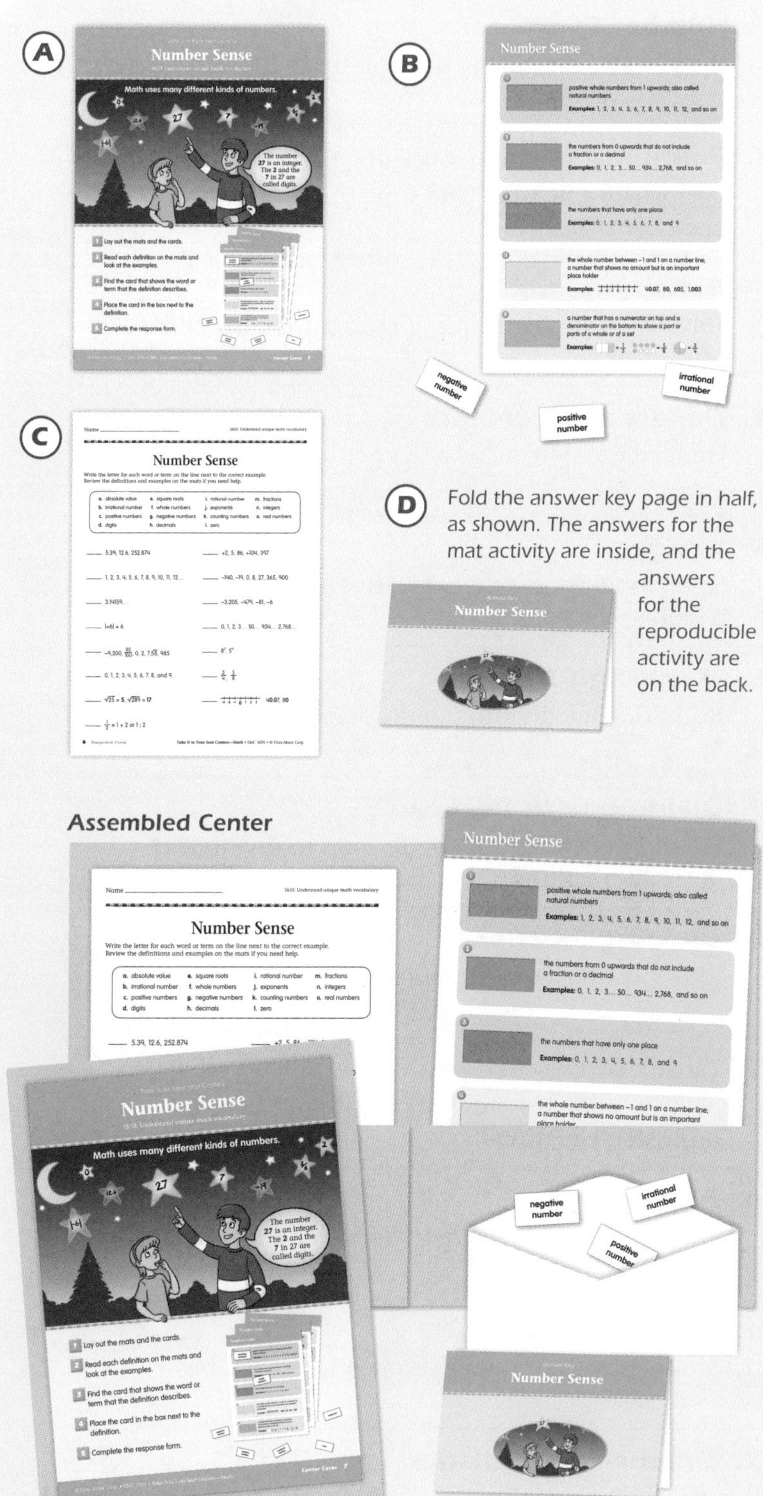

Student ______________________

Center Checklist

Center / Skill	Skill Level	Date
1. Number Sense Understand unique math vocabulary for words and terms that describe numbers		
2. Rounding and Estimation Use place value understanding to round numbers and make estimates		
3. Ratio and Rate Solve word problems using ratio (function) tables and unit rates		
4. Dollars and Percents Understand percent as a fraction of 100		
5. Integers Apply understanding of positive and negative integers to solve word problems		
6. Multi-Digit Division Build fluency dividing multi-digit numbers		
7. Dividing with Decimals Extend understanding of division to divide with decimal fractions		
8. Dividing Fractions Multiply and divide fractions and mixed numbers		
9. Order of Operations Use the standard order of operations to solve multistep equations		
10. Algebra Use variables in algebraic expressions and equations		
11. Complex Figures Find perimeters and areas of complex figures		
12. Graphs and Statistics Use graphs and plots to organize and display statistical data		

Number Sense

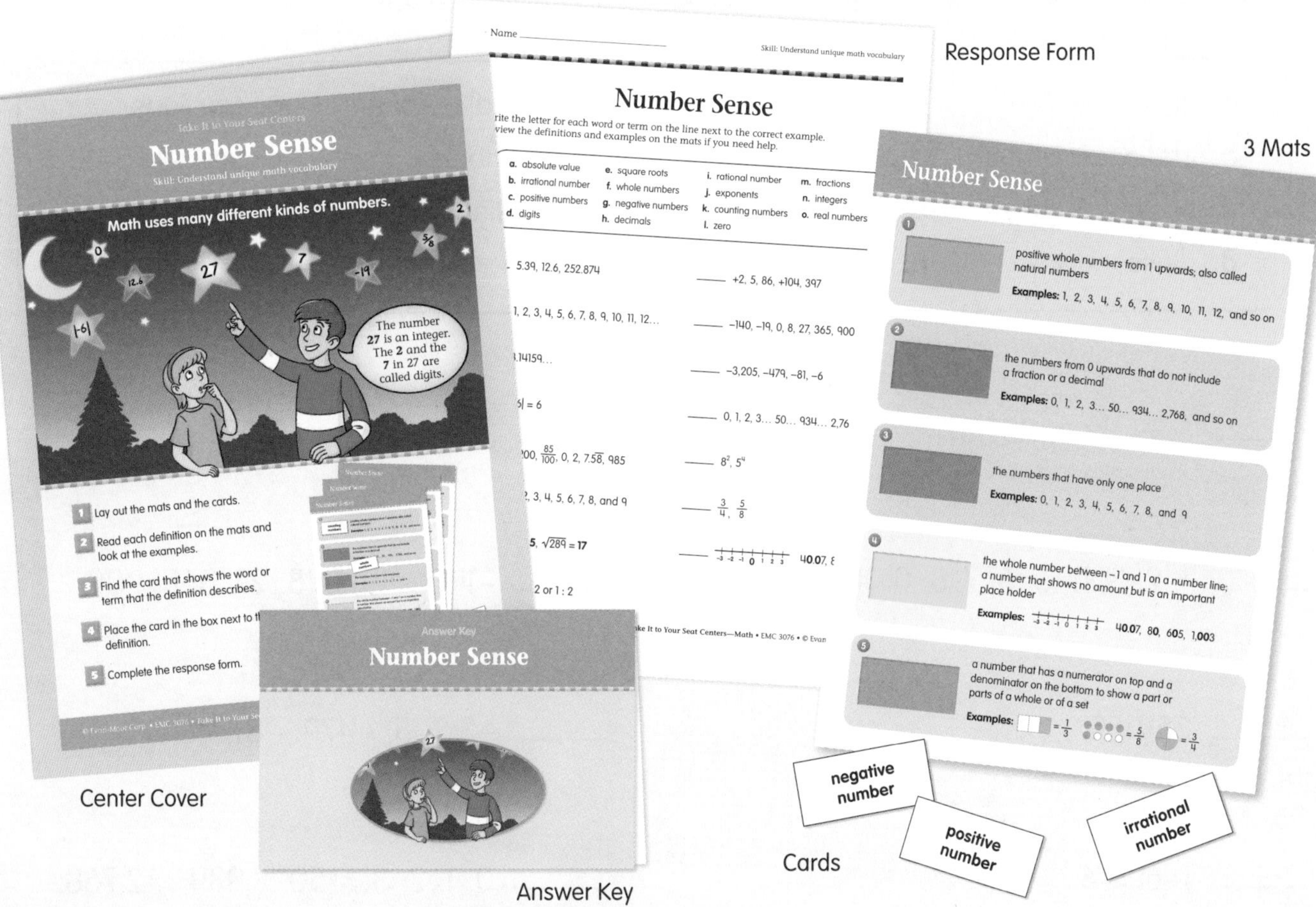

Skill: Understand unique math vocabulary for words and terms that describe numbers

Steps to Follow

1. **Prepare the center.** (See page 3.)
2. **Introduce the center.** State the goal. Say: *You will read definitions of different kinds of numbers and find the correct word or term each definition describes.*
3. **Teach the skill.** Demonstrate how to use the center with individual students or small groups.
4. **Practice the skill.** Have students use the center independently or with a partner.

Contents

Name ______________________________

Number Sense

Write the letter for each word or term on the line next to the correct example. Review the definitions and examples on the mats if you need help.

a. absolute value	**e.** square roots	**i.** rational number	**m.** fractions
b. irrational number	**f.** whole numbers	**j.** exponents	**n.** integers
c. positive numbers	**g.** negative numbers	**k.** counting numbers	**o.** real numbers
d. digits	**h.** decimals	**l.** zero	

_____ 5.39, 12.6, 252.874

_____ 1, 2, 3, 4, 5, 6, 7, 8, 9, 10, 11, 12...

_____ 3.14159...

_____ |+6| = 6

_____ $-9{,}200, \frac{85}{100}, 0, 2, 7.5\overline{8}, 985$

_____ 0, 1, 2, 3, 4, 5, 6, 7, 8, and 9

_____ $\sqrt{25} = \mathbf{5}$, $\sqrt{289} = \mathbf{17}$

_____ $\frac{1}{2} = 1 \div 2$ or 1 : 2

_____ +2, 5, 86, +104, 397

_____ –140, –19, 0, 8, 27, 365, 900

_____ –3,205, –479, –81, –6

_____ 0, 1, 2, 3... 50... 934... 2,768...

_____ $8^2, 5^4$

_____ $\frac{3}{4}, \frac{5}{8}$

_____ 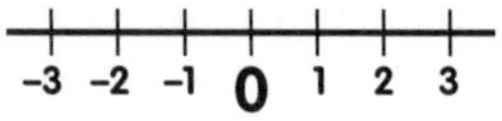

4**0.0**7, 8**0**

Number Sense

Skill: Understand unique math vocabulary

Math uses many different kinds of numbers.

0 12.6 27 7 -19 5/8 2 |-6|

The number **27** is an integer. The **2** and the **7** in 27 are called digits.

1. Lay out the mats and the cards.
2. Read each definition on the mats and look at the examples.
3. Find the card that shows the word or term that the definition describes.
4. Place the card in the box next to the definition.
5. Complete the response form.

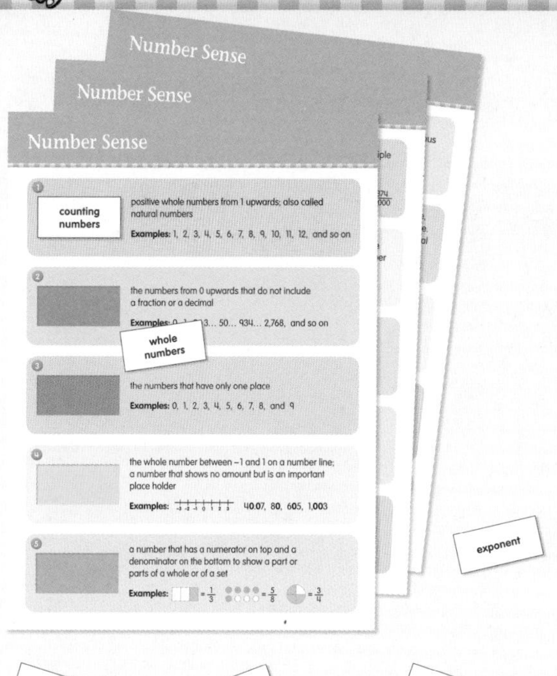

Number Sense

Answer Key

(fold)

Response Form

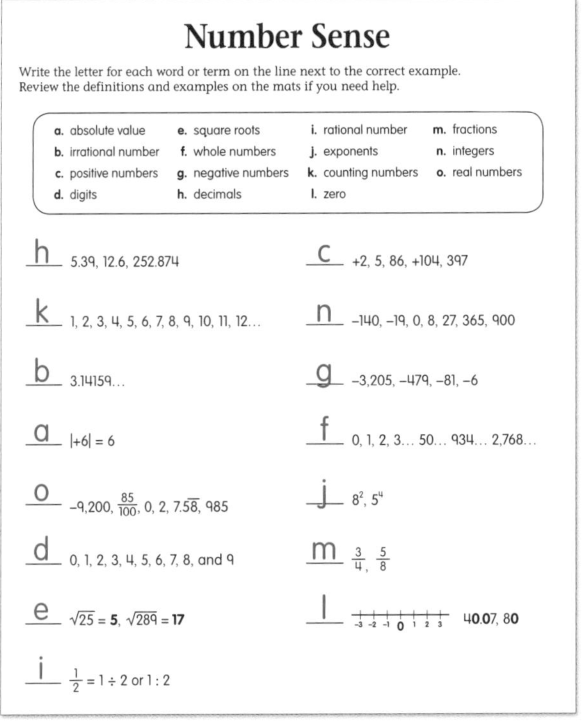

Number Sense

Write the letter for each word or term on the line next to the correct example.
Review the definitions and examples on the mats if you need help.

a. absolute value	**e.** square roots	**i.** rational number	**m.** fractions
b. irrational number	**f.** whole numbers	**j.** exponents	**n.** integers
c. positive numbers	**g.** negative numbers	**k.** counting numbers	**o.** real numbers
d. digits	**h.** decimals	**l.** zero	

h 5.39, 12.6, 252.874

c +2, 5, 86, +104, 397

k 1, 2, 3, 4, 5, 6, 7, 8, 9, 10, 11, 12...

n −140, −19, 0, 8, 27, 365, 900

b 3.14159...

g −3,205, −479, −81, −6

a |+6| = 6

f 0, 1, 2, 3... 50... 934... 2,768...

o −9,200, $\frac{85}{100}$, 0, 2, $7.\overline{58}$, 985

j 8^2, 5^4

d 0, 1, 2, 3, 4, 5, 6, 7, 8, and 9

m $\frac{3}{4}$, $\frac{5}{8}$

e $\sqrt{25}$ = **5**, $\sqrt{289}$ = **17**

l -3 -2 -1 **0** 1 2 3 4**0**.07, 8**0**

i $\frac{1}{2}$ = 1 ÷ 2 or 1 : 2

Answer Key

Number Sense

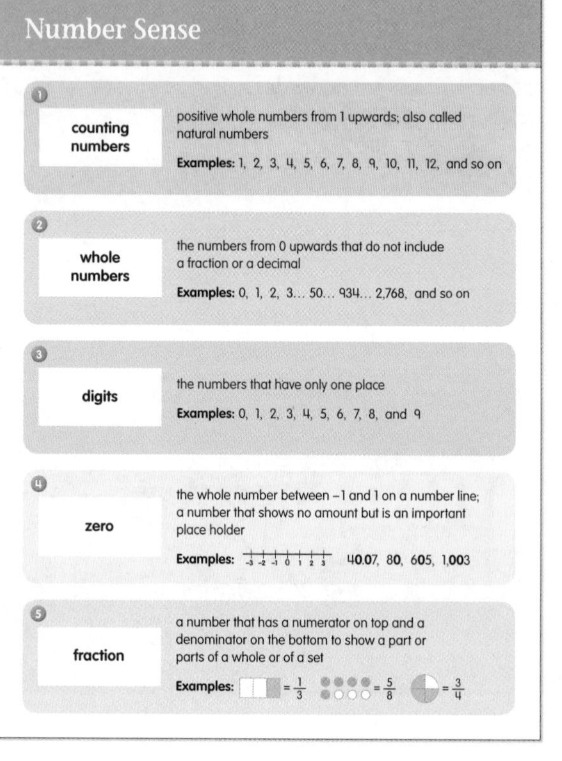

Number Sense

1 **counting numbers** — positive whole numbers from 1 upwards; also called natural numbers
Examples: 1, 2, 3, 4, 5, 6, 7, 8, 9, 10, 11, 12, and so on

2 **whole numbers** — the numbers from 0 upwards that do not include a fraction or a decimal
Examples: 0, 1, 2, 3... 50... 934... 2,768, and so on

3 **digits** — the numbers that have only one place
Examples: 0, 1, 2, 3, 4, 5, 6, 7, 8, and 9

4 **zero** — the whole number between –1 and 1 on a number line; a number that shows no amount but is an important place holder
Examples: -3 -2 -1 0 1 2 3 40.07, 80, 605, 1,003

5 **fraction** — a number that has a numerator on top and a denominator on the bottom to show a part or parts of a whole or of a set
Examples: $= \frac{1}{3}$ $= \frac{5}{8}$ $= \frac{3}{4}$

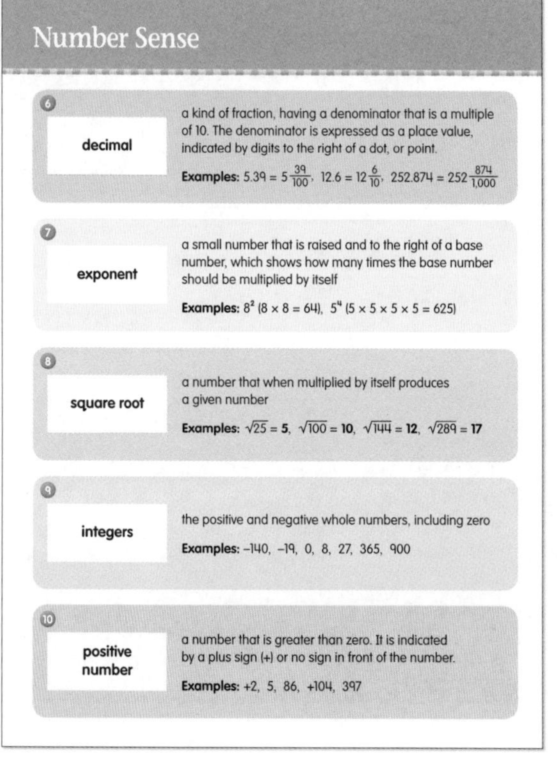

Number Sense

6 **decimal** — a kind of fraction, having a denominator that is a multiple of 10. The denominator is expressed as a place value, indicated by digits to the right of a dot, or point.
Examples: $5.39 = 5\frac{39}{100}$, $12.6 = 12\frac{6}{10}$, $252.874 = 252\frac{874}{1,000}$

7 **exponent** — a small number that is raised and to the right of a base number, which shows how many times the base number should be multiplied by itself
Examples: 8^2 (8 × 8 = 64), 5^4 (5 × 5 × 5 × 5 = 625)

8 **square root** — a number that when multiplied by itself produces a given number
Examples: $\sqrt{25}$ = **5**, $\sqrt{100}$ = **10**, $\sqrt{144}$ = **12**, $\sqrt{289}$ = **17**

9 **integers** — the positive and negative whole numbers, including zero
Examples: –140, –19, 0, 8, 27, 365, 900

10 **positive number** — a number that is greater than zero. It is indicated by a plus sign (+) or no sign in front of the number.
Examples: +2, 5, 86, +104, 397

Number Sense

11 **negative number** — a number that is less than zero. It is indicated by a minus sign (–) in front of the number.
Examples: –3,205, –479, –81, –6,

12 **absolute value** — the distance from zero for any number on a number line, regardless of whether that number is positive or negative. It is indicated by placing the number between two vertical parallel lines.
Examples: |+6| = 6, |–10.4| = 10.4 |–4| = 4 |+4| = 4 -4 -3 -2 -1 0 1 2 3 4

13 **rational number** — any number, including all integers and all fractions, that can be written as a ratio
Examples: $\frac{1}{2}$ = 1 ÷ 2 or 1 : 2, $7 = \frac{7}{1}$, $0.317 = \frac{317}{1,000}$

14 **irrational number** — any number that can be written as a decimal but not as a simple fraction or ratio; a decimal that goes on forever without repeating
Example: π (pi) 3.14159...

15 **real number** — any number on a number line, including large and small, positive and negative, whole numbers and zero, decimals and fractions, rational and irrational
Examples: –9,200, $\frac{85}{100}$, 0, 2, $7.\overline{58}$, 86.45, 985, 13,476

Number Sense

1

positive whole numbers from 1 upwards; also called natural numbers

Examples: 1, 2, 3, 4, 5, 6, 7, 8, 9, 10, 11, 12, and so on

2

the numbers from 0 upwards that do not include a fraction or a decimal

Examples: 0, 1, 2, 3... 50... 934... 2,768, and so on

3

the numbers that have only one place

Examples: 0, 1, 2, 3, 4, 5, 6, 7, 8, and 9

4

the whole number between –1 and 1 on a number line; a number that shows no amount but is an important place holder

Examples: 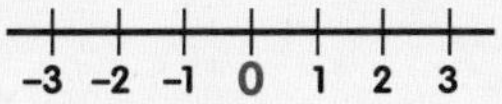 –3 –2 –1 **0** 1 2 3   4**0**.**0**7, 8**0**, 6**0**5, 1,**00**3

5

a number that has a numerator on top and a denominator on the bottom to show a part or parts of a whole or of a set

Examples: 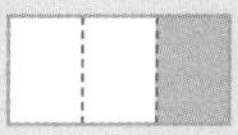 $= \frac{1}{3}$  $= \frac{5}{8}$ 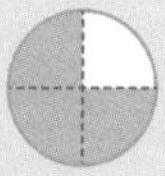 $= \frac{3}{4}$

Number Sense

6

a kind of fraction, having a denominator that is a multiple of 10. The denominator is expressed as a place value, indicated by digits to the right of a dot, or point.

Examples: $5.39 = 5\frac{39}{100}$, $12.6 = 12\frac{6}{10}$, $252.874 = 252\frac{874}{1,000}$

7

a small number that is raised and to the right of a base number, which shows how many times the base number should be multiplied by itself

Examples: 8^2 ($8 \times 8 = 64$), 5^4 ($5 \times 5 \times 5 \times 5 = 625$)

8

a number that when multiplied by itself produces a given number

Examples: $\sqrt{25} = \mathbf{5}$, $\sqrt{100} = \mathbf{10}$, $\sqrt{144} = \mathbf{12}$, $\sqrt{289} = \mathbf{17}$

9

the positive and negative whole numbers, including zero

Examples: –140, –19, 0, 8, 27, 365, 900

10

a number that is greater than zero. It is indicated by a plus sign (+) or no sign in front of the number.

Examples: +2, 5, 86, +104, 397

Number Sense

11

a number that is less than zero. It is indicated by a minus sign (–) in front of the number.

Examples: –3,205, –479, –81, –6,

12

the distance from zero for any number on a number line, regardless of whether that number is positive or negative. It is indicated by placing the number between two vertical parallel lines.

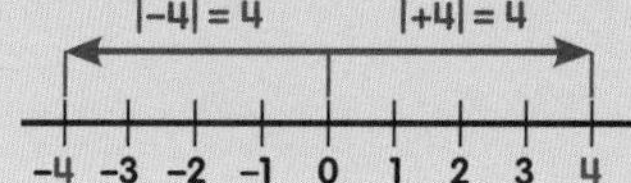

Examples: $|+6| = 6$, $|-10.4| = 10.4$

13

any number, including all integers and all fractions, that can be written as a ratio

Examples: $\frac{1}{2} = 1 \div 2$ or $1 : 2$, $7 = \frac{7}{1}$, $0.317 = \frac{317}{1,000}$

14

any number that can be written as a decimal but not as a simple fraction or ratio; a decimal that goes on forever without repeating

Example: π (pi) 3.14159...

15

any number on a number line, including large and small, positive and negative, whole numbers and zero, decimals and fractions, rational and irrational

Examples: –9,200, $\frac{85}{100}$, 0, 2, $7.\overline{58}$, 86.45, 985, 13,476

counting numbers	whole numbers	digits
fraction	decimal	exponent
integers	positive number	negative number
rational number	irrational number	real number
zero	square root	absolute value

Number Sense EMC 3076 © Evan-Moor Corp.	Number Sense EMC 3076 © Evan-Moor Corp.	Number Sense EMC 3076 © Evan-Moor Corp.
Number Sense EMC 3076 © Evan-Moor Corp.	Number Sense EMC 3076 © Evan-Moor Corp.	Number Sense EMC 3076 © Evan-Moor Corp.
Number Sense EMC 3076 © Evan-Moor Corp.	Number Sense EMC 3076 © Evan-Moor Corp.	Number Sense EMC 3076 © Evan-Moor Corp.
Number Sense EMC 3076 © Evan-Moor Corp.	Number Sense EMC 3076 © Evan-Moor Corp.	Number Sense EMC 3076 © Evan-Moor Corp.
Number Sense EMC 3076 © Evan-Moor Corp.	Number Sense EMC 3076 © Evan-Moor Corp.	Number Sense EMC 3076 © Evan-Moor Corp.

Take It to Your Seat Centers

Rounding and Estimation

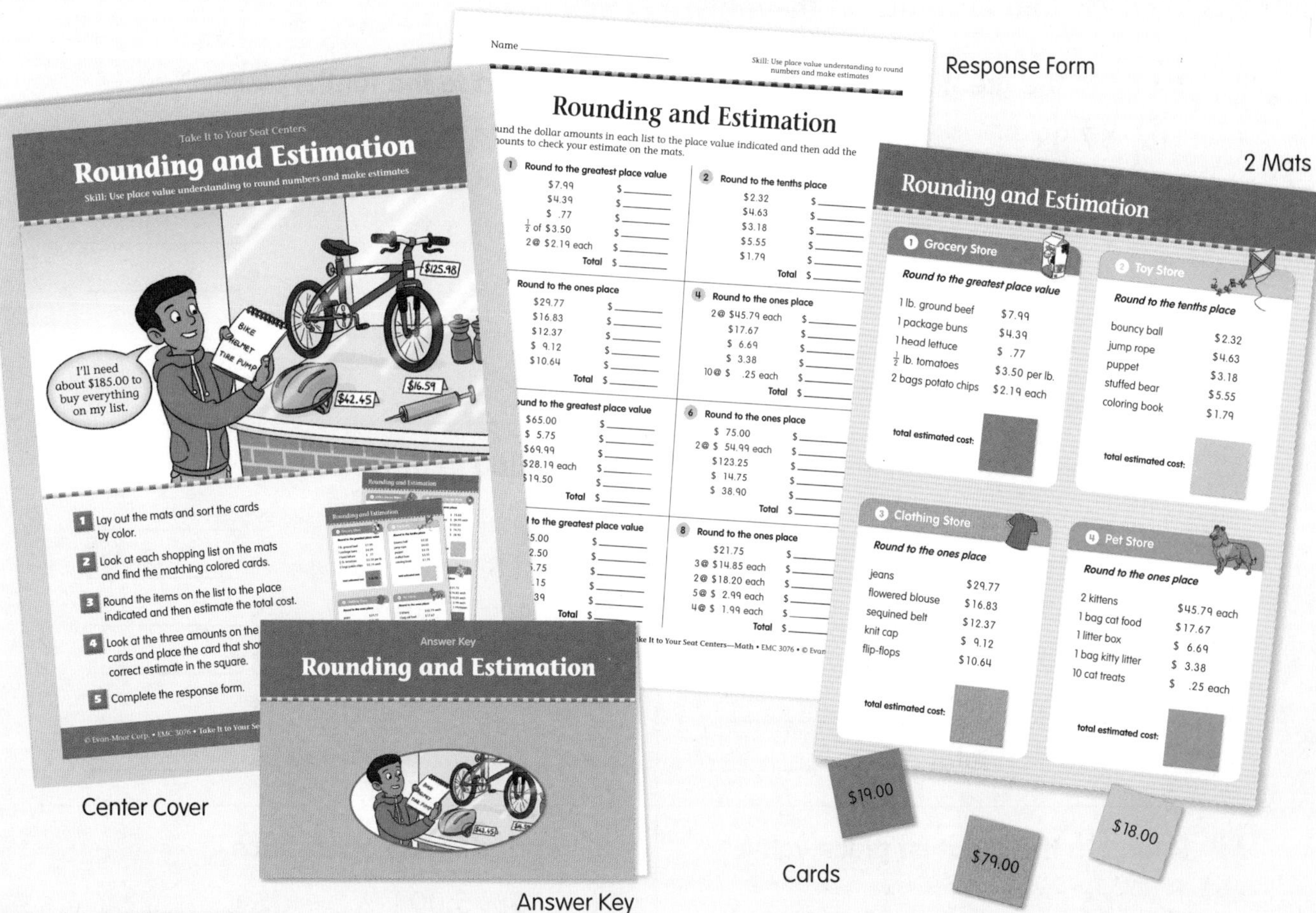

Skill: Use place value understanding to round numbers and make estimates

Steps to Follow

1. **Prepare the center.** (See page 3.)
2. **Introduce the center.** State the goal. Say: *You will round the prices of the items on each shopping list on the mats and then estimate the total cost of the items.*
3. **Teach the skill.** Demonstrate how to use the center with individual students or small groups.
4. **Practice the skill.** Have students use the center independently or with a partner.

Contents

Name ______________________

Skill: Use place value understanding to round numbers and make estimates

Rounding and Estimation

Round the dollar amounts in each list to the place value indicated and then add the amounts to check your estimate on the mats.

1 Round to the greatest place value

$7.99	$ ________
$4.39	$ ________
$ .77	$ ________
$\frac{1}{2}$ of $3.50	$ ________
2@ $2.19 each	$ ________
Total	$ ________

2 Round to the tenths place

$2.32	$ ________
$4.63	$ ________
$3.18	$ ________
$5.55	$ ________
$1.79	$ ________
Total	$ ________

3 Round to the ones place

$29.77	$ ________
$16.83	$ ________
$12.37	$ ________
$ 9.12	$ ________
$10.64	$ ________
Total	$ ________

4 Round to the ones place

2@ $45.79 each	$ ________
$17.67	$ ________
$ 6.69	$ ________
$ 3.38	$ ________
10@ $ .25 each	$ ________
Total	$ ________

5 Round to the greatest place value

$65.00	$ ________
$ 5.75	$ ________
$69.99	$ ________
3@ $28.19 each	$ ________
$19.50	$ ________
Total	$ ________

6 Round to the ones place

$ 75.00	$ ________
2@ $ 54.99 each	$ ________
$123.25	$ ________
$ 14.75	$ ________
$ 38.90	$ ________
Total	$ ________

7 Round to the greatest place value

$45.00	$ ________
$12.50	$ ________
$25.75	$ ________
$ 2.15	$ ________
$ 3.39	$ ________
Total	$ ________

8 Round to the ones place

$21.75	$ ________
3@ $14.85 each	$ ________
2@ $18.20 each	$ ________
5@ $ 2.99 each	$ ________
4@ $ 1.99 each	$ ________
Total	$ ________

Rounding and Estimation

Skill: Use place value understanding to round numbers and make estimates

1. Lay out the mats and sort the cards by color.
2. Look at each shopping list on the mats and find the matching colored cards.
3. Round the items on the list to the place indicated and then estimate the total cost.
4. Look at the three amounts on the colored cards and place the card that shows the correct estimate in the square.
5. Complete the response form.

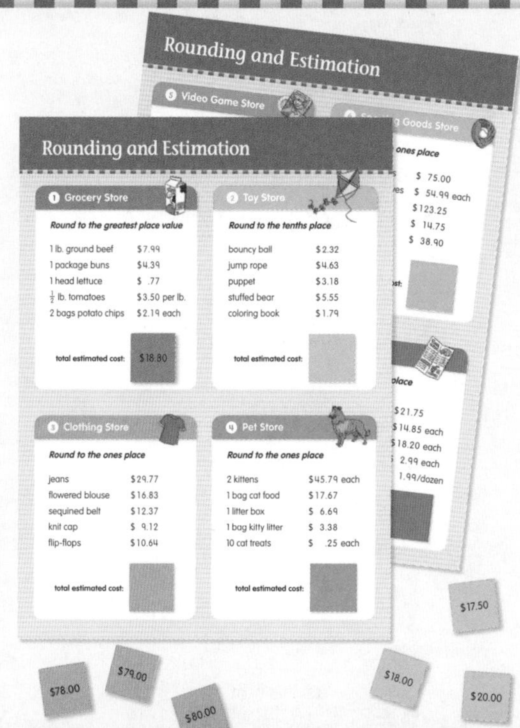

Rounding and Estimation

Answer Key

(fold)

Response Form

Rounding and Estimation

Round the dollar amounts in each list to the place value indicated and then add the amounts to check your estimate on the mats.

1 Round to the greatest place value

Amount	Rounded
$7.99	$ 8.00
$4.39	$ 4.00
$ .77	$ 0.80
$\frac{1}{2}$ of $3.50	$ 2.00
2@ $2.19 each	$ 4.00
Total	$ 18.80

2 Round to the tenths place

Amount	Rounded
$2.32	$ 2.30
$4.63	$ 4.60
$3.18	$ 3.20
$5.55	$ 5.60
$1.79	$ 1.80
Total	$ 17.50

3 Round to the ones place

Amount	Rounded
$29.77	$ 30.00
$16.83	$ 17.00
$12.37	$ 12.00
$ 9.12	$ 9.00
$10.64	$ 11.00
Total	$ 79.00

4 Round to the ones place

Amount	Rounded
2@ $45.79 each	$ 92.00
$17.67	$ 18.00
$ 6.69	$ 7.00
$ 3.38	$ 3.00
10@ $ .25 each	$ 3.00
Total	$ 123.00

5 Round to the greatest place value

Amount	Rounded
$65.00	$ 70.00
$ 5.75	$ 6.00
$69.99	$ 70.00
3@ $28.19 each	$ 90.00
$19.50	$ 20.00
Total	$ 256.00

6 Round to the ones place

Amount	Rounded
$ 75.00	$ 75.00
2@ $ 54.99 each	$ 110.00
$123.25	$ 123.00
$ 14.75	$ 15.00
$ 38.90	$ 39.00
Total	$ 362.00

7 Round to the greatest place value

Amount	Rounded
$45.00	$ 50.00
$12.50	$ 10.00
$25.75	$ 30.00
$ 2.15	$ 2.00
$ 3.39	$ 3.00
Total	$ 95.00

8 Round to the ones place

Amount	Rounded
$21.75	$ 22.00
3@ $14.85 each	$ 45.00
2@ $18.20 each	$ 36.00
5@ $ 2.99 each	$ 15.00
4@ $ 1.99 each	$ 8.00
Total	$ 126.00

Answer Key

Rounding and Estimation

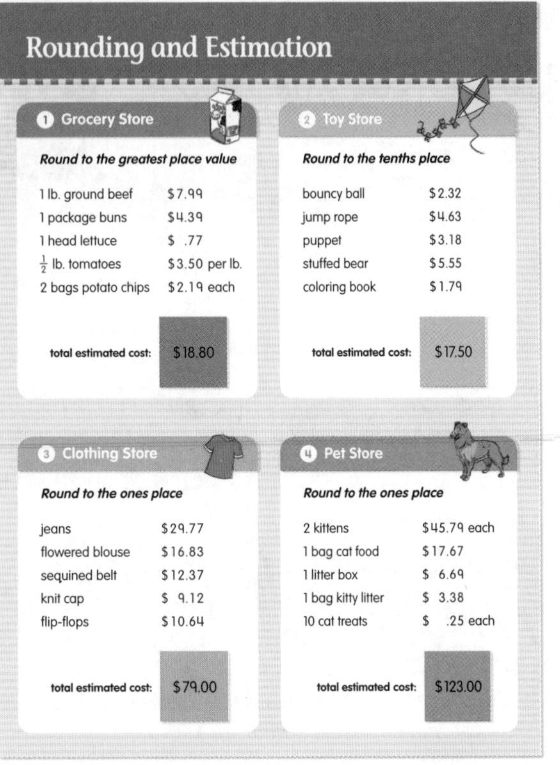

Rounding and Estimation

1 Grocery Store

Round to the greatest place value

1 lb. ground beef	$7.99
1 package buns	$4.39
1 head lettuce	$ .77
$\frac{1}{2}$ lb. tomatoes	$3.50 per lb.
2 bags potato chips	$2.19 each

total estimated cost: $18.80

2 Toy Store

Round to the tenths place

bouncy ball	$2.32
jump rope	$4.63
puppet	$3.18
stuffed bear	$5.55
coloring book	$1.79

total estimated cost: $17.50

3 Clothing Store

Round to the ones place

jeans	$29.77
flowered blouse	$16.83
sequined belt	$12.37
knit cap	$ 9.12
flip-flops	$10.64

total estimated cost: $79.00

4 Pet Store

Round to the ones place

2 kittens	$45.79 each
1 bag cat food	$17.67
1 litter box	$ 6.69
1 bag kitty litter	$ 3.38
10 cat treats	$ .25 each

total estimated cost: $123.00

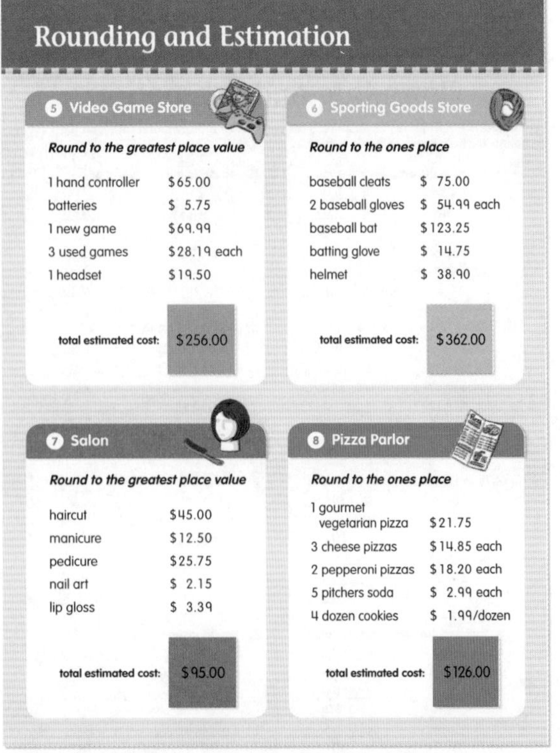

Rounding and Estimation

5 Video Game Store

Round to the greatest place value

1 hand controller	$65.00
batteries	$ 5.75
1 new game	$69.99
3 used games	$28.19 each
1 headset	$19.50

total estimated cost: $256.00

6 Sporting Goods Store

Round to the ones place

baseball cleats	$ 75.00
2 baseball gloves	$ 54.99 each
baseball bat	$123.25
batting glove	$ 14.75
helmet	$ 38.90

total estimated cost: $362.00

7 Salon

Round to the greatest place value

haircut	$45.00
manicure	$12.50
pedicure	$25.75
nail art	$ 2.15
lip gloss	$ 3.39

total estimated cost: $95.00

8 Pizza Parlor

Round to the ones place

1 gourmet vegetarian pizza	$21.75
3 cheese pizzas	$14.85 each
2 pepperoni pizzas	$18.20 each
5 pitchers soda	$ 2.99 each
4 dozen cookies	$ 1.99/dozen

total estimated cost: $126.00

Rounding and Estimation

 Grocery Store

Round to the greatest place value

1 lb. ground beef	$7.99
1 package buns	$4.39
1 head lettuce	$ .77
$\frac{1}{2}$ lb. tomatoes	$3.50 per lb.
2 bags potato chips	$2.19 each

total estimated cost:

 Toy Store

Round to the tenths place

bouncy ball	$2.32
jump rope	$4.63
puppet	$3.18
stuffed bear	$5.55
coloring book	$1.79

total estimated cost:

 Clothing Store

Round to the ones place

jeans	$29.77
flowered blouse	$16.83
sequined belt	$12.37
knit cap	$ 9.12
flip-flops	$10.64

total estimated cost:

 Pet Store

Round to the ones place

2 kittens	$45.79 each
1 bag cat food	$17.67
1 litter box	$ 6.69
1 bag kitty litter	$ 3.38
10 cat treats	$ .25 each

total estimated cost:

Rounding and Estimation

5 Video Game Store

Round to the greatest place value

1 hand controller	$65.00
batteries	$ 5.75
1 new game	$69.99
3 used games	$28.19 each
1 headset	$19.50

total estimated cost:

6 Sporting Goods Store

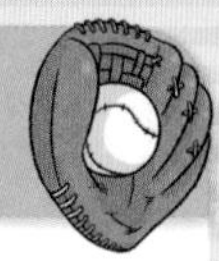

Round to the ones place

baseball cleats	$ 75.00
2 baseball gloves	$ 54.99 each
baseball bat	$123.25
batting glove	$ 14.75
helmet	$ 38.90

total estimated cost:

7 Salon

Round to the greatest place value

haircut	$45.00
manicure	$12.50
pedicure	$25.75
nail art	$ 2.15
lip gloss	$ 3.39

total estimated cost:

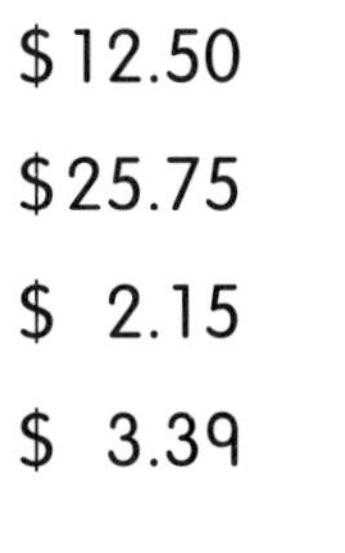

8 Pizza Parlor

Round to the ones place

1 gourmet vegetarian pizza	$21.75
3 cheese pizzas	$14.85 each
2 pepperoni pizzas	$18.20 each
5 pitchers soda	$ 2.99 each
4 dozen cookies	$ 1.99 /dozen

total estimated cost:

$18.80	$19.00	$20.00
$17.50	$18.00	$20.00
$79.00	$78.00	$80.00
$123.00	$120.00	$125.00
$ 256.00	$250.00	$300.00
$362.00	$360.00	$400.00
$95.00	$89.00	$100.00
$126.00	$125.00	$130.00

Rounding and Estimation EMC 3076 © Evan-Moor Corp.	Rounding and Estimation EMC 3076 © Evan-Moor Corp.	Rounding and Estimation EMC 3076 © Evan-Moor Corp.
Rounding and Estimation EMC 3076 © Evan-Moor Corp.	Rounding and Estimation EMC 3076 © Evan-Moor Corp.	Rounding and Estimation EMC 3076 © Evan-Moor Corp.
Rounding and Estimation EMC 3076 © Evan-Moor Corp.	Rounding and Estimation EMC 3076 © Evan-Moor Corp.	Rounding and Estimation EMC 3076 © Evan-Moor Corp.
Rounding and Estimation EMC 3076 © Evan-Moor Corp.	Rounding and Estimation EMC 3076 © Evan-Moor Corp.	Rounding and Estimation EMC 3076 © Evan-Moor Corp.
Rounding and Estimation EMC 3076 © Evan-Moor Corp.	Rounding and Estimation EMC 3076 © Evan-Moor Corp.	Rounding and Estimation EMC 3076 © Evan-Moor Corp.
Rounding and Estimation EMC 3076 © Evan-Moor Corp.	Rounding and Estimation EMC 3076 © Evan-Moor Corp.	Rounding and Estimation EMC 3076 © Evan-Moor Corp.
Rounding and Estimation EMC 3076 © Evan-Moor Corp.	Rounding and Estimation EMC 3076 © Evan-Moor Corp.	Rounding and Estimation EMC 3076 © Evan-Moor Corp.
Rounding and Estimation EMC 3076 © Evan-Moor Corp.	Rounding and Estimation EMC 3076 © Evan-Moor Corp.	Rounding and Estimation EMC 3076 © Evan-Moor Corp.

Take It to Your Seat Centers

Ratio and Rate

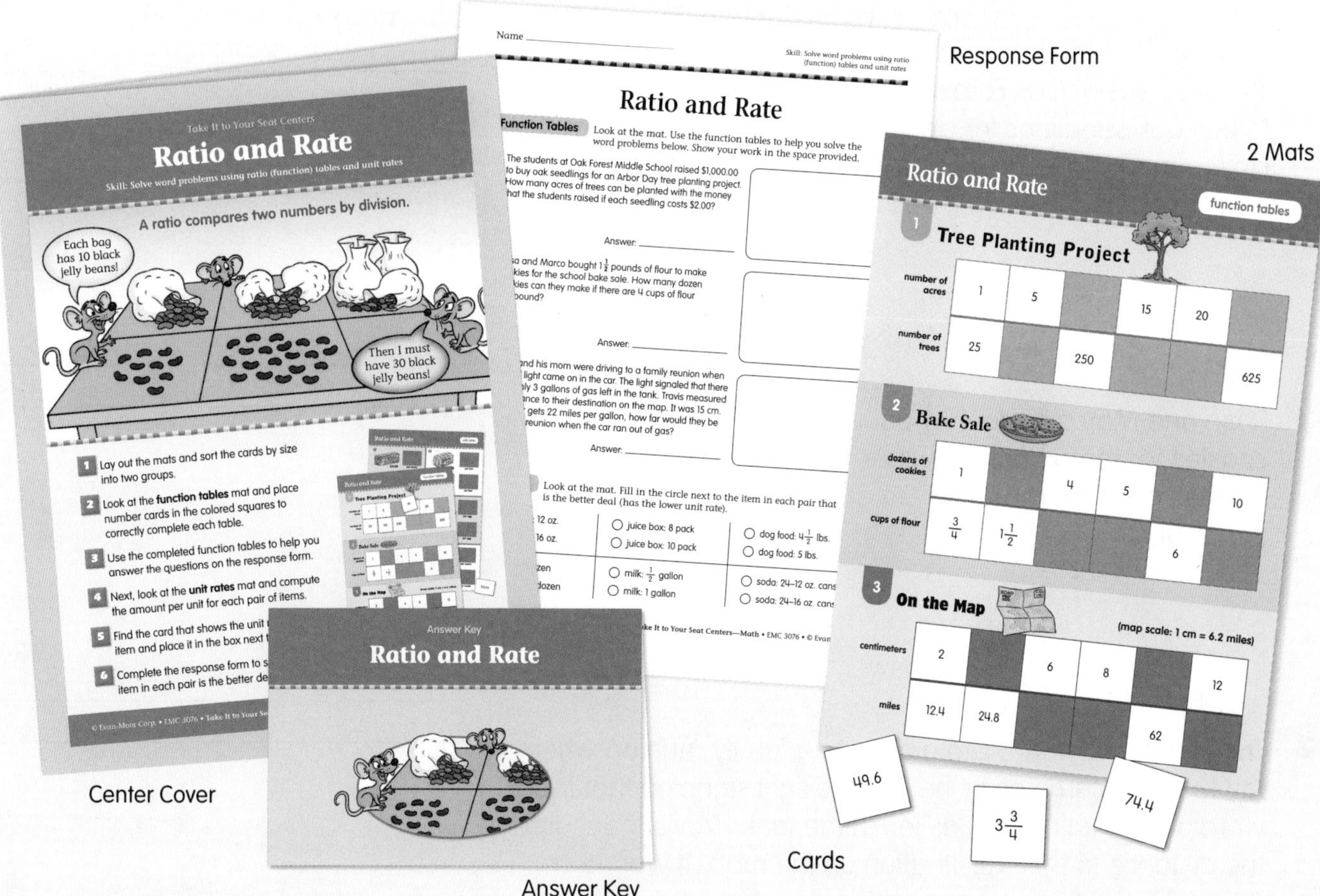

Skill: Solve word problems using ratio (function) tables and unit rates

Steps to Follow

1. **Prepare the center.** (See page 3.)
2. **Introduce the center.** State the goal. Say: *You will complete tables of ratios and compute unit rates and then use the information to solve word problems.*
3. **Teach the skill.** Demonstrate how to use the center with individual students or small groups.
4. **Practice the skill.** Have students use the center independently or with a partner.

Contents

Name ____________________

Skill: Solve word problems using ratio (function) tables and unit rates

Ratio and Rate

Function Tables Look at the mat. Use the function tables to help you solve the word problems below. Show your work in the space provided.

1. The students at Oak Forest Middle School raised $1,000.00 to buy oak seedlings for an Arbor Day tree planting project. How many acres of trees can be planted with the money that the students raised if each seedling costs $2.00?

   Answer: ____________________

2. Rosa and Marco bought $1\frac{1}{2}$ pounds of flour to make cookies for the school bake sale. How many dozen cookies can they make if there are 4 cups of flour per pound?

   Answer: ____________________

3. Travis and his mom were driving to a family reunion when the fuel light came on in the car. The light signaled that there were only 3 gallons of gas left in the tank. Travis measured the distance to their destination on the map. It was 15 cm. If the car gets 22 miles per gallon, how far would they be from the reunion when the car ran out of gas?

   Answer: ____________________

Unit Rates Look at the mat. Fill in the circle next to the item in each pair that is the better deal (has the lower unit rate).

○ crackers: 12 oz. ○ crackers: 16 oz.	○ juice box: 8 pack ○ juice box: 10 pack	○ dog food: $4\frac{1}{2}$ lbs. ○ dog food: 5 lbs.
○ eggs: 1 dozen ○ eggs: $1\frac{1}{2}$ dozen	○ milk: $\frac{1}{2}$ gallon ○ milk: 1 gallon	○ soda: 24–12 oz. cans ○ soda: 24–16 oz. cans

Ratio and Rate

Skill: Solve word problems using ratio (function) tables and unit rates

1. Lay out the mats and sort the cards by size into two groups.
2. Look at the **function tables** mat and place number cards in the colored squares to correctly complete each table.
3. Use the completed function tables to help you answer the questions on the response form.
4. Next, look at the **unit rates** mat and compute the amount per unit for each pair of items.
5. Find the card that shows the unit rate of each item and place it in the box next to the item.
6. Complete the response form to show which item in each pair is the better deal.

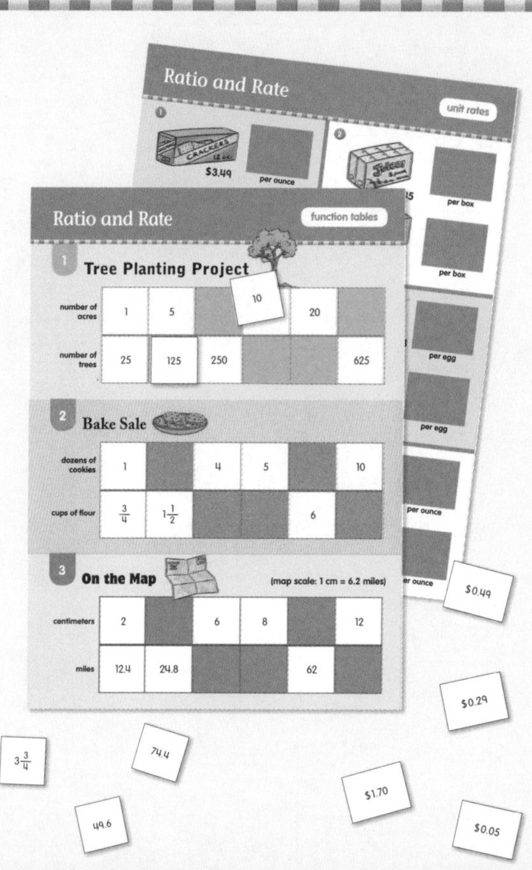

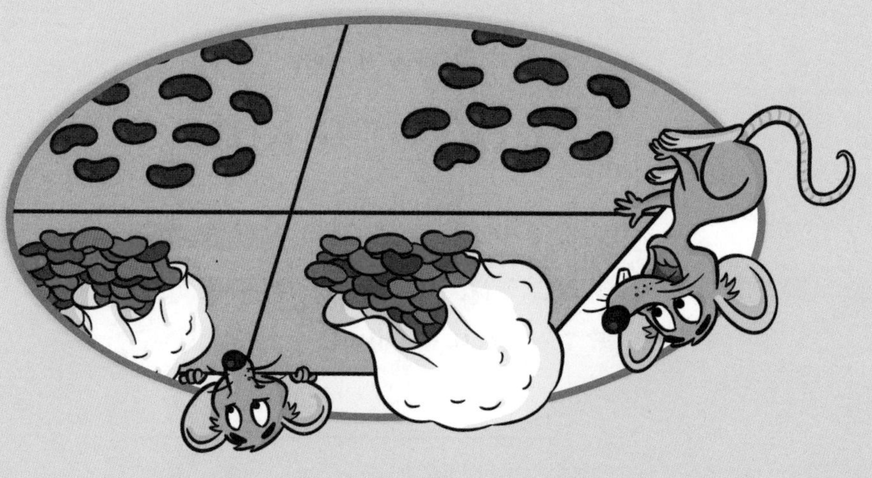

Ratio and Rate

Answer Key

(fold)

Response Form

Ratio and Rate

Function Tables Look at the mat. Use the function tables to help you solve the word problems below. Show your work in the space provided.

1. The students at Oak Forest Middle School raised $1,000.00 to buy oak seedlings for an Arbor Day tree planting project. How many acres of trees can be planted with the money that the students raised if each seedling costs $2.00?

   Answer: 20 acres

2. Rosa and Marco bought $1\frac{1}{2}$ pounds of flour to make cookies for the school bake sale. How many dozen cookies can they make if there are 4 cups of flour per pound?

   Answer: 8 dozen

3. Travis and his mom were driving to a family reunion when the fuel light came on in the car. The light signaled that there were only 3 gallons of gas left in the tank. Travis measured the distance to their destination on the map. It was 15 cm. If the car gets 22 miles per gallon, how far would they be from the reunion when the car ran out of gas?

   Answer: 27 miles

Unit Rates Look at the mat. Fill in the circle next to the item in each pair that is the better deal (has the lower unit rate).

○ crackers: 12 oz. ● crackers: 16 oz.	● juice box: 8 pack ○ juice box: 10 pack	○ dog food: $4\frac{1}{2}$ lbs. ● dog food: 5 lbs.
● eggs: 1 dozen ○ eggs: $1\frac{1}{2}$ dozen	○ milk: $\frac{1}{2}$ gallon ● milk: 1 gallon	○ soda: 24–12 oz. cans ● soda: 24–16 oz. cans

Answer Key

Ratio and Rate

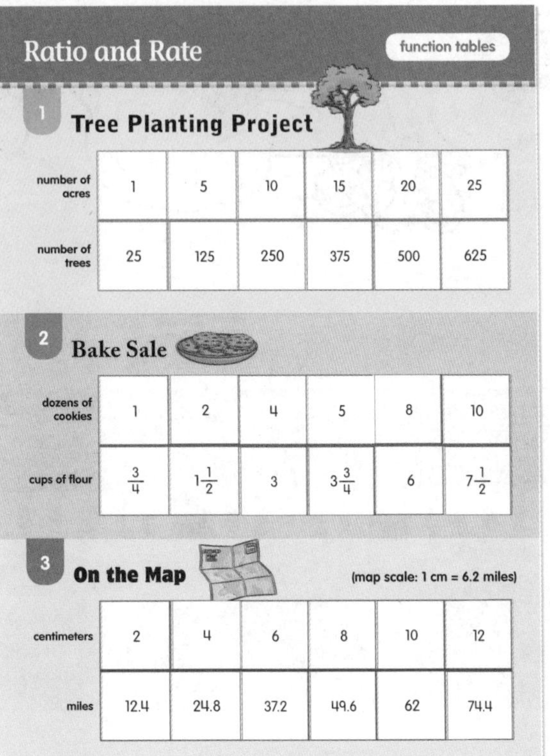

Ratio and Rate — function tables

1 Tree Planting Project

number of acres	1	5	10	15	20	25
number of trees	25	125	250	375	500	625

2 Bake Sale

dozens of cookies	1	2	4	5	8	10
cups of flour	$\frac{3}{4}$	$1\frac{1}{2}$	3	$3\frac{3}{4}$	6	$7\frac{1}{2}$

3 On the Map (map scale: 1 cm = 6.2 miles)

centimeters	2	4	6	8	10	12
miles	12.4	24.8	37.2	49.6	62	74.4

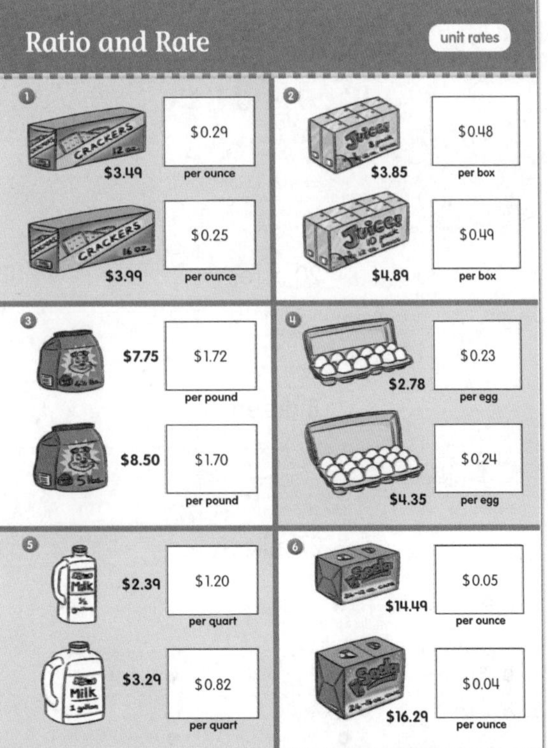

Ratio and Rate — unit rates

1. $3.49 — $0.29 per ounce; $3.99 — $0.25 per ounce
2. $3.85 — $0.48 per box; $4.89 — $0.49 per box
3. $7.75 — $1.72 per pound; $8.50 — $1.70 per pound
4. $2.78 — $0.23 per egg; $4.35 — $0.24 per egg
5. $2.39 — $1.20 per quart; $3.29 — $0.82 per quart
6. $14.49 — $0.05 per ounce; $16.29 — $0.04 per ounce

1 Tree Planting Project

number of acres	1	5		15	20	
number of trees	25		250			625

2 Bake Sale

dozens of cookies	1		4	5		10
cups of flour	$\frac{3}{4}$	$1\frac{1}{2}$			6	

3 On the Map

(map scale: 1 cm = 6.2 miles)

centimeters	2		6	8		12
miles	12.4	24.8			62	

Ratio and Rate

unit rates

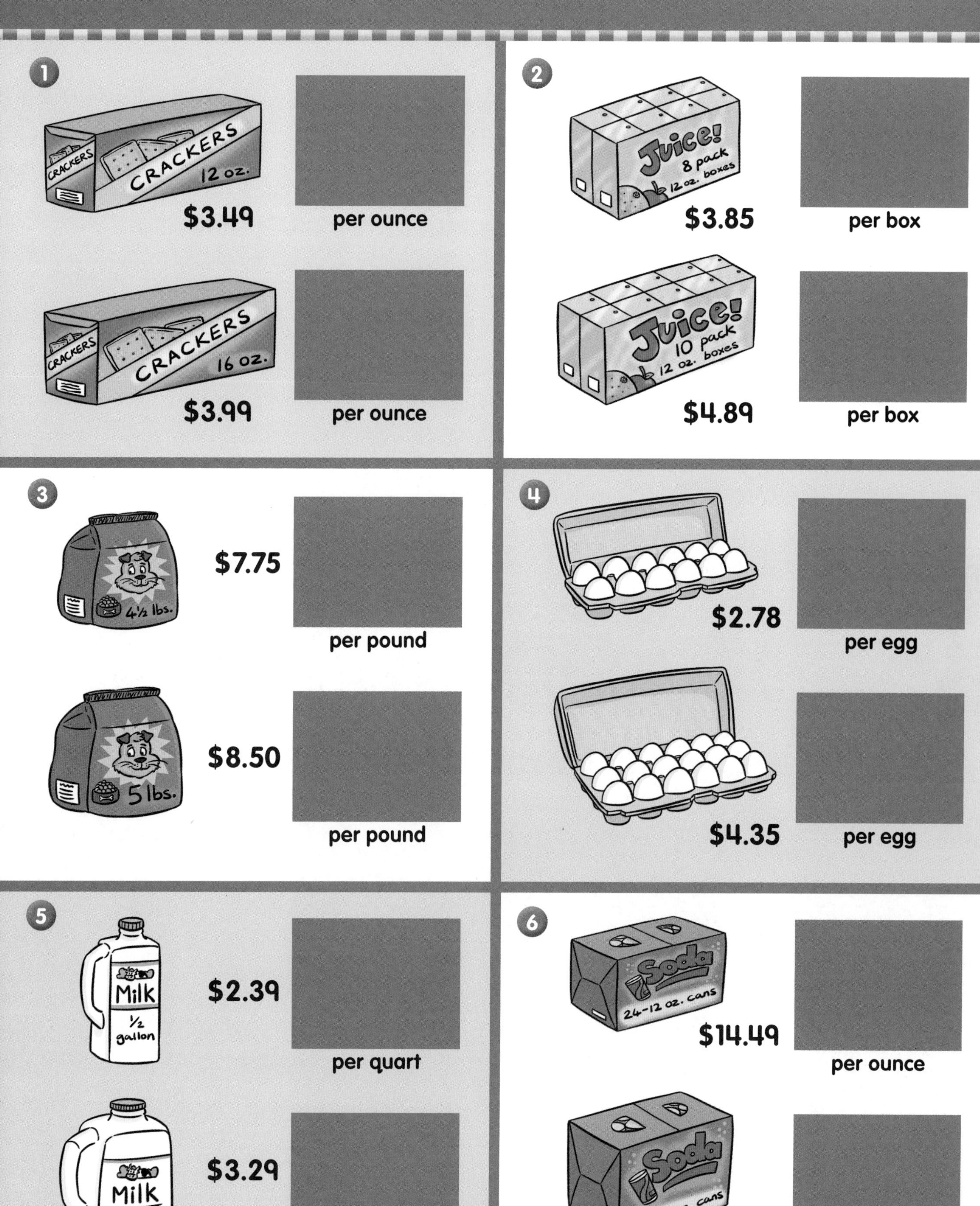

10	25	125	$0.29	$0.25
375	500	2	$0.48	$0.49
8	3	$3\frac{3}{4}$	$1.70	$1.72
$7\frac{1}{2}$	4	10	$0.23	$0.24
37.2	49.6	74.4	$1.20	$0.82
			$0.04	$0.05

Ratio and Rate
EMC 3076
© Evan-Moor Corp.

Ratio and Rate
EMC 3076
© Evan-Moor Corp.

Ratio and Rate
EMC 3076
© Evan-Moor Corp.

Ratio and Rate
EMC 3076
© Evan-Moor Corp.

Ratio and Rate
EMC 3076
© Evan-Moor Corp.

Ratio and Rate
EMC 3076
© Evan-Moor Corp.

Ratio and Rate
EMC 3076
© Evan-Moor Corp.

Ratio and Rate
EMC 3076
© Evan-Moor Corp.

Ratio and Rate
EMC 3076
© Evan-Moor Corp.

Ratio and Rate
EMC 3076
© Evan-Moor Corp.

Ratio and Rate
EMC 3076
© Evan-Moor Corp.

Ratio and Rate
EMC 3076
© Evan-Moor Corp.

Ratio and Rate
EMC 3076
© Evan-Moor Corp.

Ratio and Rate
EMC 3076
© Evan-Moor Corp.

Ratio and Rate
EMC 3076
© Evan-Moor Corp.

Ratio and Rate
EMC 3076
© Evan-Moor Corp.

Ratio and Rate
EMC 3076
© Evan-Moor Corp.

Ratio and Rate
EMC 3076
© Evan-Moor Corp.

Ratio and Rate
EMC 3076
© Evan-Moor Corp.

Ratio and Rate
EMC 3076
© Evan-Moor Corp.

Ratio and Rate
EMC 3076
© Evan-Moor Corp.

Ratio and Rate
EMC 3076
© Evan-Moor Corp.

Ratio and Rate
EMC 3076
© Evan-Moor Corp.

Ratio and Rate
EMC 3076
© Evan-Moor Corp.

Ratio and Rate
EMC 3076
© Evan-Moor Corp.

Ratio and Rate
EMC 3076
© Evan-Moor Corp.

Ratio and Rate
EMC 3076
© Evan-Moor Corp.

Take It to Your Seat Centers

Dollars and Percents

Skill: Understand percent as a fraction of 100

Steps to Follow

1. **Prepare the center.** (See page 3.)
2. **Introduce the center.** State the goal. Say: *You will use dollar amounts, fractions, and percents to compute the discount for each item on the mats.*
3. **Teach the skill.** Demonstrate how to use the center with individual students or small groups.
4. **Practice the skill.** Have students use the center independently or with a partner.

Contents

Name ____________________ Skill: Understand percent as a fraction of 100

Dollars and Percents

Look at the mats. Calculate the sale price (final cost) for each item and write it on the line next to the item's number.

1 $________ 2 $________ 3 $________ 4 $________

5 $________ 6 $________ 7 $________ 8 $________

9 $________ 10 $________ 11 $________ 12 $________

Write each percent below as a fraction of 100 and fill in the correct number of squares on the 100 frame.

10% = $\frac{10}{100}$

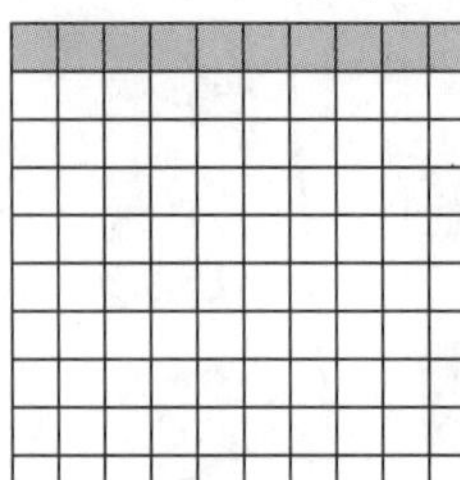

30% = ______

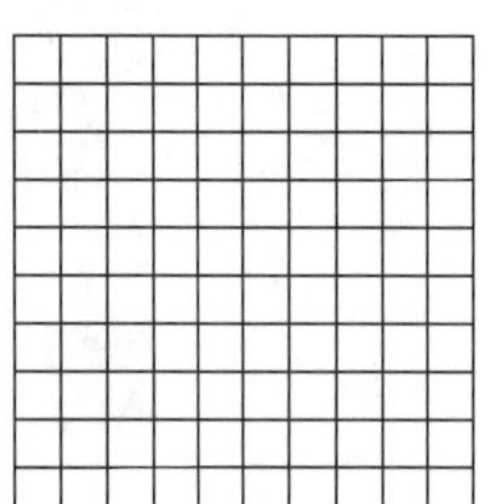

63% = ______

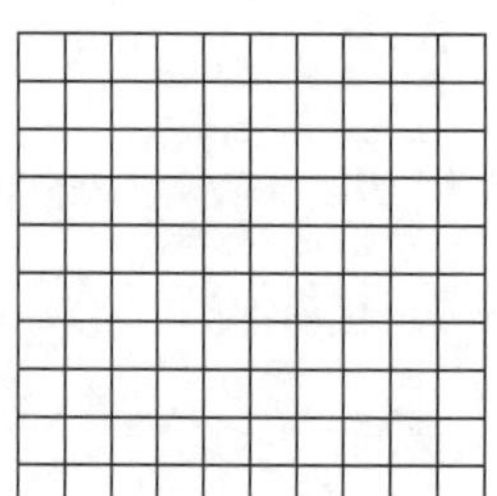

49% = ______

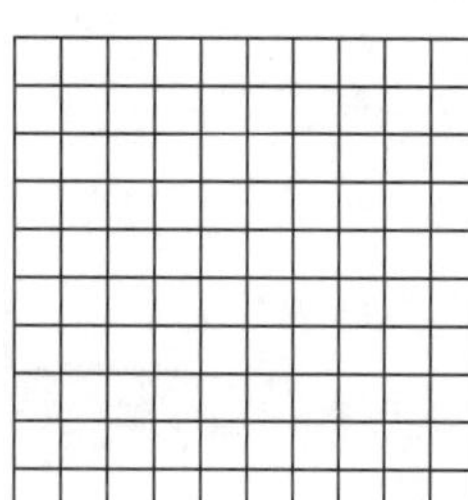

28% = ______

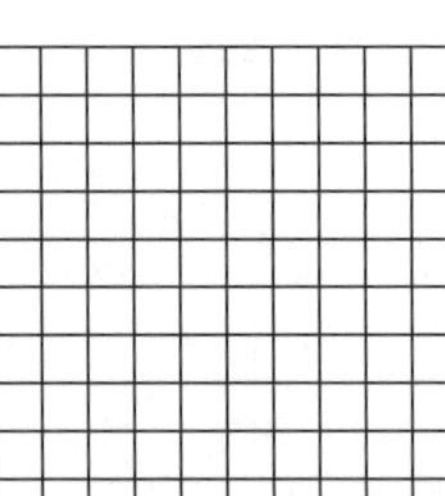

81% = ______

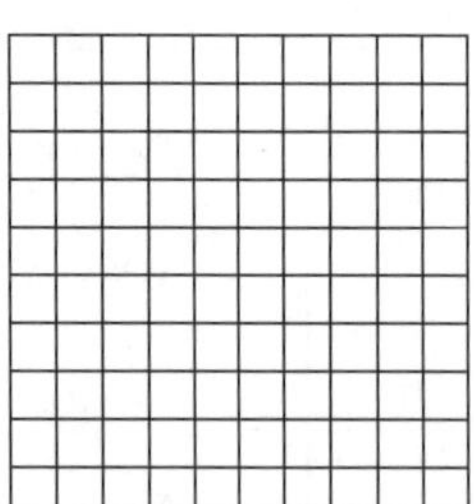

7% = ______

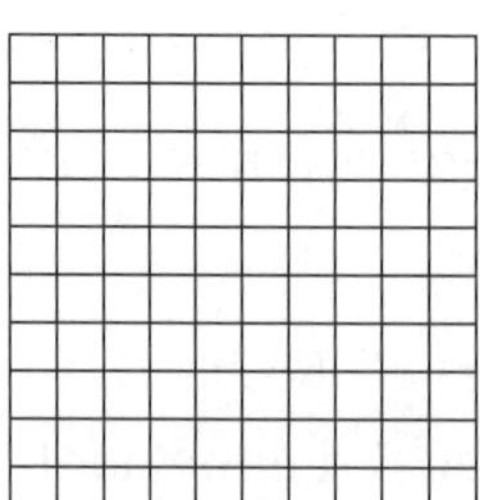

52% = ______

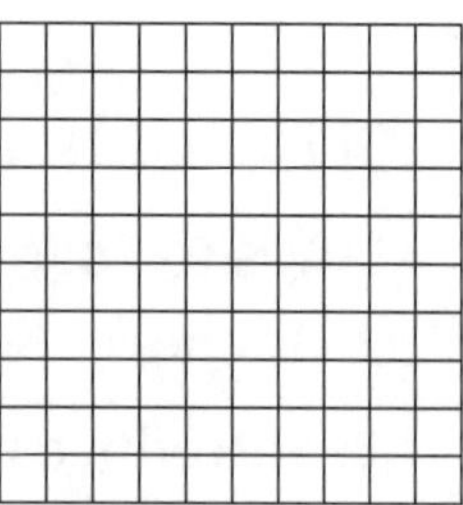

Write the fraction for each percent in its simplest form.

5% = $\frac{5}{100}$ = $\frac{1}{20}$ 40% = $\frac{40}{100}$ = ______   60% = $\frac{60}{100}$ = ______   20% = $\frac{20}{100}$ = ______

50% = $\frac{50}{100}$ = ______   75% = $\frac{75}{100}$ = ______   25% = $\frac{25}{100}$ = ______   55% = $\frac{55}{100}$ = ______

Take It to Your Seat Centers

Dollars and Percents

Skill: Understand percent as a fraction of 100

A percent is a fraction of 100.

$$50\% = \frac{50}{100} = \frac{1}{2}$$

1. Lay out the mats and the cards.
2. Read the price tag for each item on the mats.
3. Use the percent-, fraction-, or dollars-off amount to compute the amount or percent of the discount for each item.
4. Find the card that shows the correct amount or percent and place it in the box.
5. Complete the response form.

Dollars and Percents

Answer Key

(fold)

Response Form

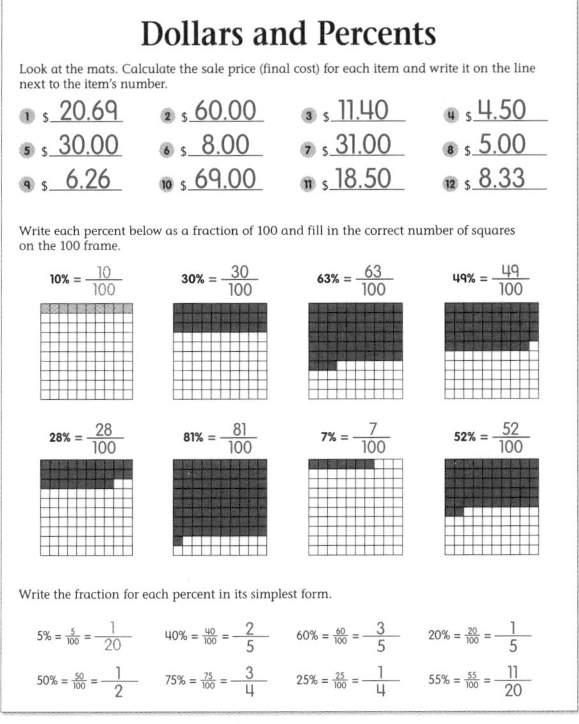

Dollars and Percents

Look at the mats. Calculate the sale price (final cost) for each item and write it on the line next to the item's number.

1. $ 20.69
2. $ 60.00
3. $ 11.40
4. $ 4.50
5. $ 30.00
6. $ 8.00
7. $ 31.00
8. $ 5.00
9. $ 6.26
10. $ 69.00
11. $ 18.50
12. $ 8.33

Write each percent below as a fraction of 100 and fill in the correct number of squares on the 100 frame.

10% = $\frac{10}{100}$ **30%** = $\frac{30}{100}$ **63%** = $\frac{63}{100}$ **49%** = $\frac{49}{100}$

28% = $\frac{28}{100}$ **81%** = $\frac{81}{100}$ **7%** = $\frac{7}{100}$ **52%** = $\frac{52}{100}$

Write the fraction for each percent in its simplest form.

$5\% = \frac{5}{100} = \frac{1}{20}$ $40\% = \frac{40}{100} = \frac{2}{5}$ $60\% = \frac{60}{100} = \frac{3}{5}$ $20\% = \frac{20}{100} = \frac{1}{5}$

$50\% = \frac{50}{100} = \frac{1}{2}$ $75\% = \frac{75}{100} = \frac{3}{4}$ $25\% = \frac{25}{100} = \frac{1}{4}$ $55\% = \frac{55}{100} = \frac{11}{20}$

Answer Key

Dollars and Percents

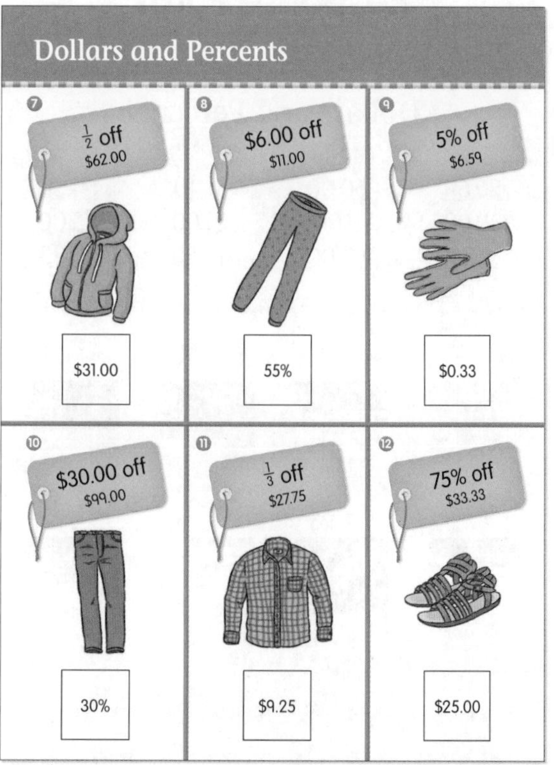

Dollars and Percents

1

amount

2

percent

3

amount

4

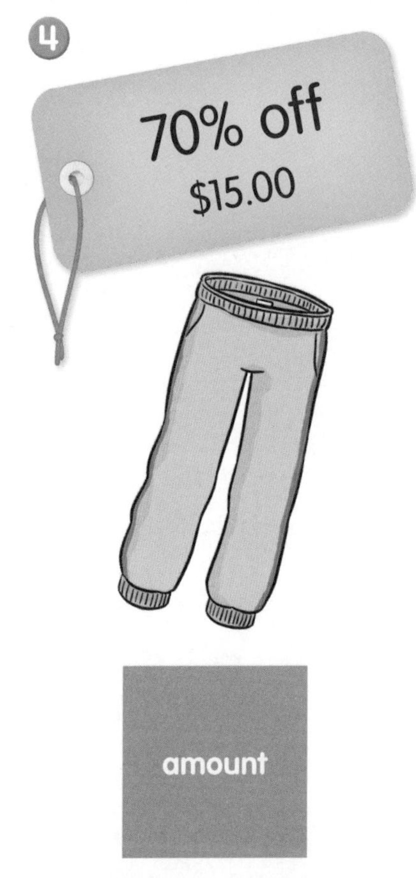

amount

5

amount

6

percent

Dollars and Percents

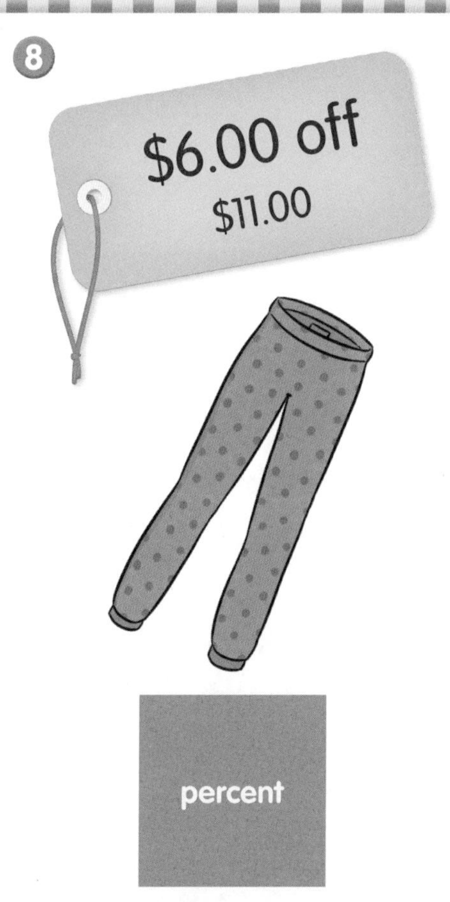

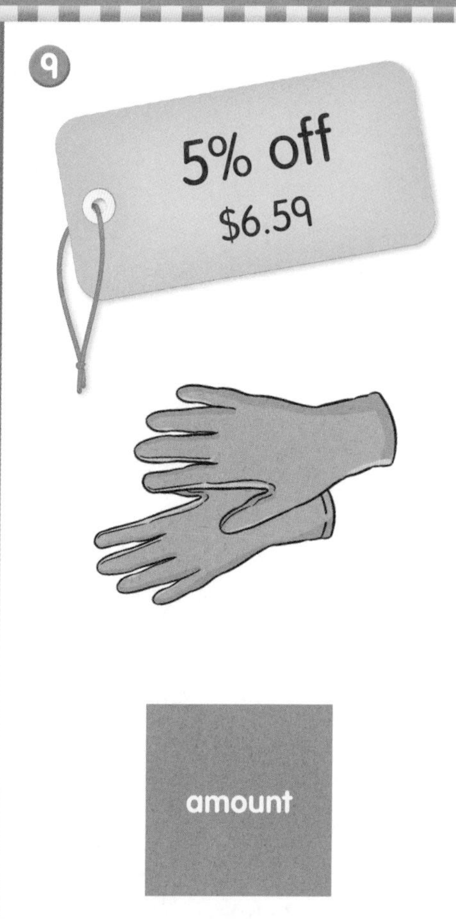

10%	15%	20%	25%
30%	35%	40%	55%
60%	65%	70%	75%
\$0.33	\$0.53	\$0.76	\$2.30
\$2.77	\$2.99	\$7.50	\$7.60
\$8.33	\$9.25	\$10.00	\$10.50
\$16.00	\$25.00	\$30.50	\$31.00

Dollars and Percents EMC 3076 © Evan-Moor Corp.	Dollars and Percents EMC 3076 © Evan-Moor Corp.	Dollars and Percents EMC 3076 © Evan-Moor Corp.	Dollars and Percents EMC 3076 © Evan-Moor Corp.
Dollars and Percents EMC 3076 © Evan-Moor Corp.	Dollars and Percents EMC 3076 © Evan-Moor Corp.	Dollars and Percents EMC 3076 © Evan-Moor Corp.	Dollars and Percents EMC 3076 © Evan-Moor Corp.
Dollars and Percents EMC 3076 © Evan-Moor Corp.	Dollars and Percents EMC 3076 © Evan-Moor Corp.	Dollars and Percents EMC 3076 © Evan-Moor Corp.	Dollars and Percents EMC 3076 © Evan-Moor Corp.
Dollars and Percents EMC 3076 © Evan-Moor Corp.	Dollars and Percents EMC 3076 © Evan-Moor Corp.	Dollars and Percents EMC 3076 © Evan-Moor Corp.	Dollars and Percents EMC 3076 © Evan-Moor Corp.
Dollars and Percents EMC 3076 © Evan-Moor Corp.	Dollars and Percents EMC 3076 © Evan-Moor Corp.	Dollars and Percents EMC 3076 © Evan-Moor Corp.	Dollars and Percents EMC 3076 © Evan-Moor Corp.
Dollars and Percents EMC 3076 © Evan-Moor Corp.	Dollars and Percents EMC 3076 © Evan-Moor Corp.	Dollars and Percents EMC 3076 © Evan-Moor Corp.	Dollars and Percents EMC 3076 © Evan-Moor Corp.
Dollars and Percents EMC 3076 © Evan-Moor Corp.	Dollars and Percents EMC 3076 © Evan-Moor Corp.	Dollars and Percents EMC 3076 © Evan-Moor Corp.	Dollars and Percents EMC 3076 © Evan-Moor Corp.

Integers

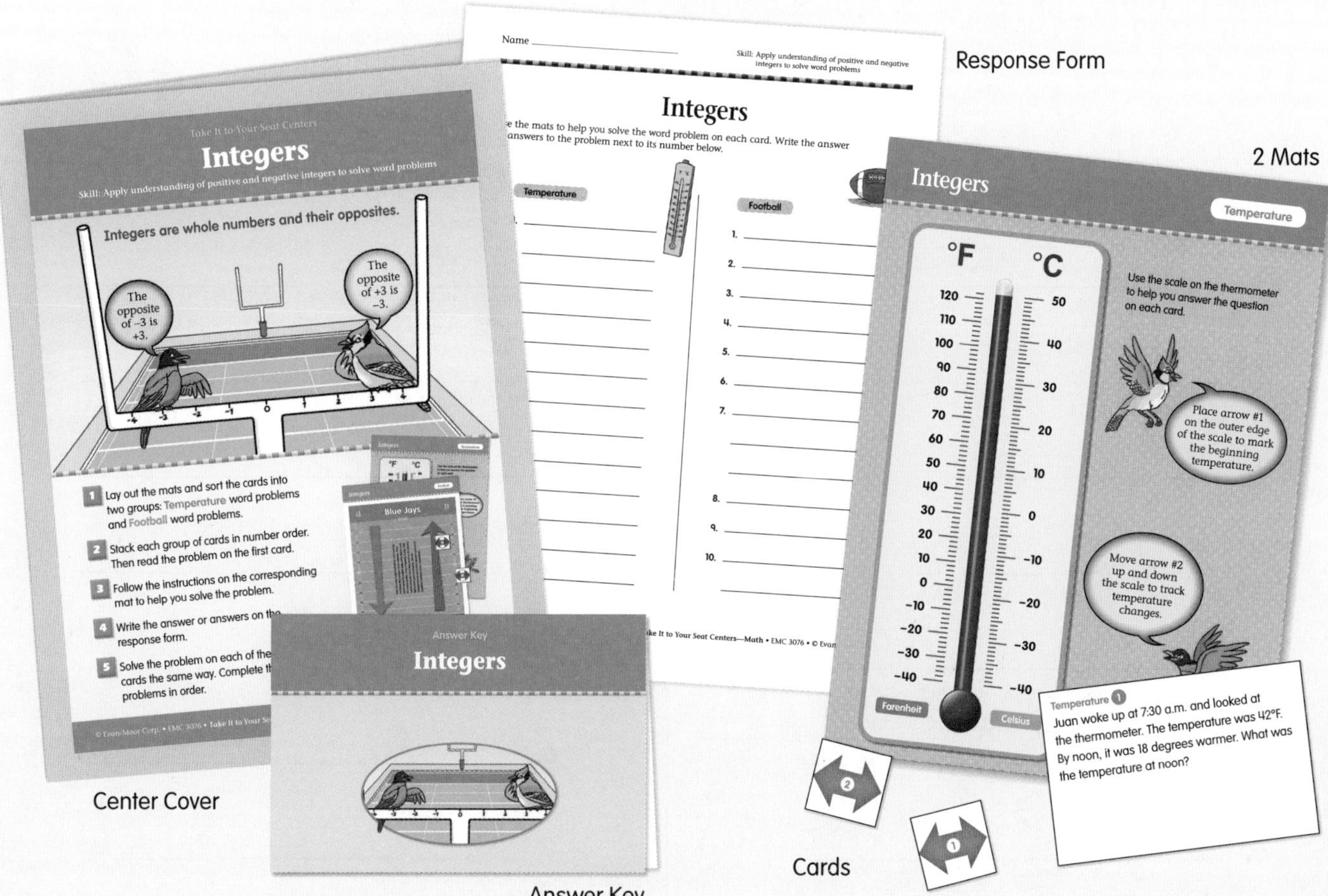

Skill: Apply understanding of positive and negative integers to solve word problems

Steps to Follow

1. **Prepare the center.** (See page 3.)
2. **Introduce the center.** State the goal. Say: *You will solve word problems, using temperatures on a thermometer or yard lines on a football field.*
3. **Teach the skill.** Demonstrate how to use the center with individual students or small groups.
4. **Practice the skill.** Have students use the center independently or with a partner.

Contents

Name ____________________

Skill: Apply understanding of positive and negative integers to solve word problems

Integers

Use the mats to help you solve the word problem on each card. Write the answer or answers to the problem next to its number below.

Temperature

1. ____________________
2. ____________________
3. ____________________
   ____
4. ____________________
5. ____________________
6. ____________________
7. ____________________
8. ____________________
   ____
9. ____________________
10. ____________________
    ____

Football

1. ____________________
2. ____________________
3. ____________________
4. ____________________
5. ____________________
6. ____________________
7. ____________________
   ____
   ____
8. ____________________
9. ____________________
10. ____________________
    ____

Integers

Skill: Apply understanding of positive and negative integers to solve word problems

Integers are whole numbers and their opposites.

The opposite of –3 is +3.

The opposite of +3 is –3.

-4 -3 -2 -1 0 1 2 3 4

1. Lay out the mats and sort the cards into two groups: **Temperature** word problems and **Football** word problems.
2. Stack each group of cards in number order. Then read the problem on the first card.
3. Follow the instructions on the corresponding mat to help you solve the problem.
4. Write the answer or answers on the response form.
5. Solve the problem on each of the other cards the same way. Complete the problems in order.

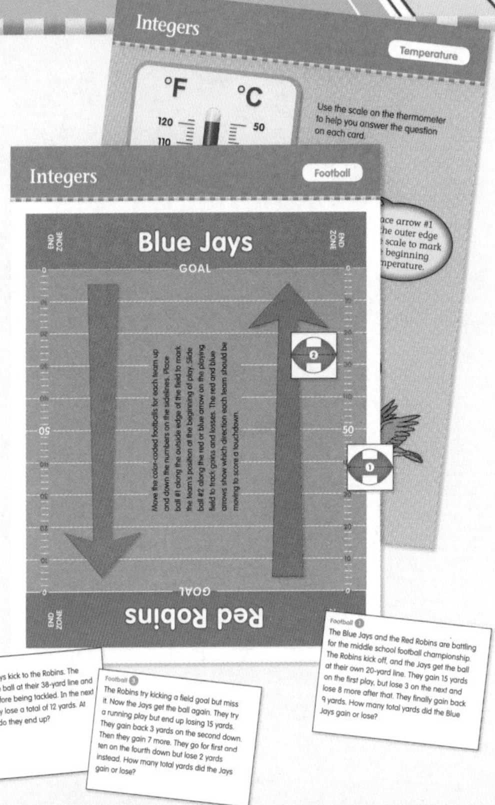

Integers

Answer Key

(fold)

Response Form

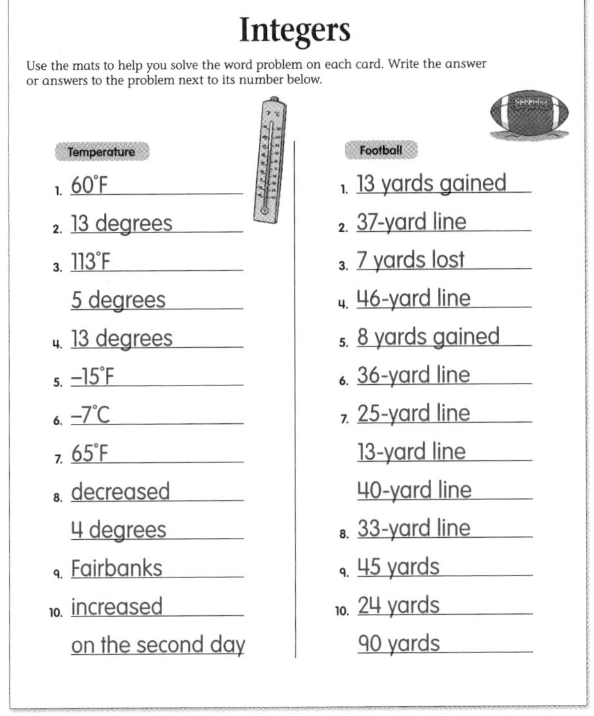

Integers

Use the mats to help you solve the word problem on each card. Write the answer or answers to the problem next to its number below.

Temperature

1. 60°F
2. 13 degrees
3. 113°F
   5 degrees
4. 13 degrees
5. –15°F
6. –7°C
7. 65°F
8. decreased
   4 degrees
9. Fairbanks
10. increased
    on the second day

Football

1. 13 yards gained
2. 37-yard line
3. 7 yards lost
4. 46-yard line
5. 8 yards gained
6. 36-yard line
7. 25-yard line
   13-yard line
   40-yard line
8. 33-yard line
9. 45 yards
10. 24 yards
    90 yards

Integers

Sample Mats

(for how to play)

Temperature

°F °C

Use the scale on the thermometer to help you answer the question on each card.

Place arrow #1 on the outer edge of the scale to mark the beginning temperature.

Move arrow #2 up and down the scale to track temperature changes.

Farenheit Celsius

Temperature 1

Juan woke up at 7:30 a.m. and looked at the thermometer. The temperature was 42°F. By noon, it was 18 degrees warmer. What was the temperature at noon?

Answer: 60°F

Football

Red Robins

Blue Jays

Move the color-coded footballs for each team up and down the numbers on the sidelines. Place ball #1 along the outside edge of the field to mark the team's position at the beginning of play. Slide ball #2 along the red or blue arrow on the playing field to track gains and losses. The red and blue arrows show which direction each team should be moving to score a touchdown.

Football 1

The Blue Jays and the Red Robins are battling for the middle school football championship. The Robins kick off, and the Jays get the ball at their own 20-yard line. They gain 15 yards on the first play, but lose 3 on the next and lose 8 more after that. They finally gain back 9 yards. How many total yards did the Blue Jays gain or lose?

Answer:
13 yards gained

Integers

Temperature

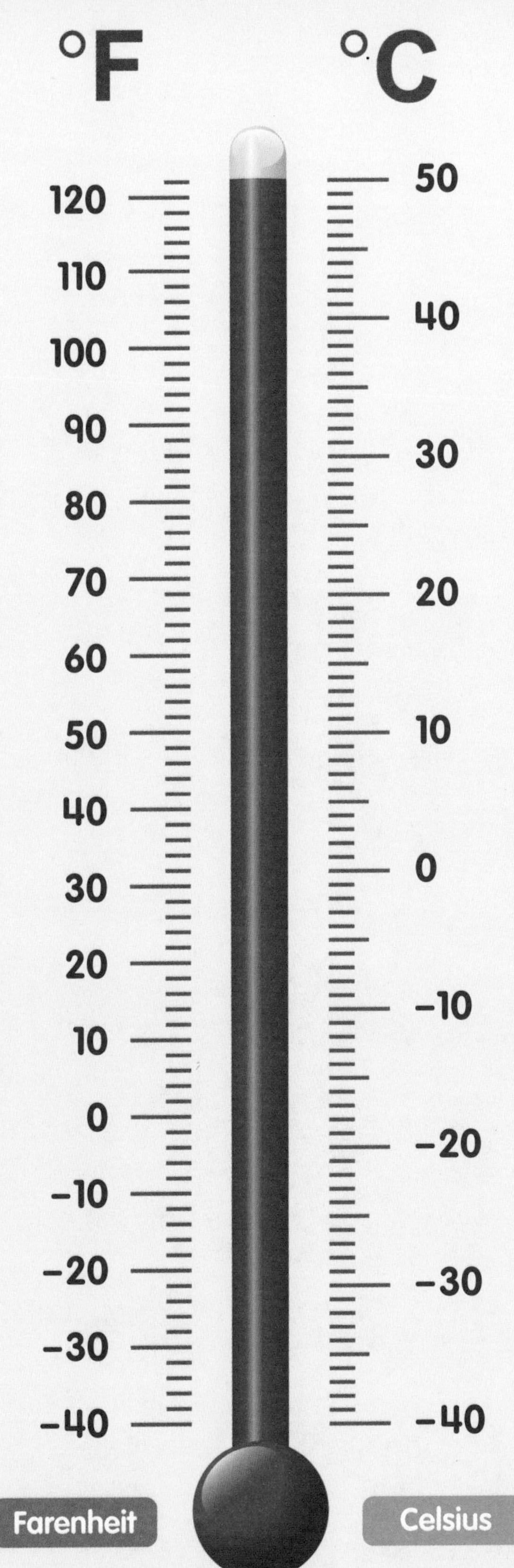

Use the scale on the thermometer to help you answer the question on each card.

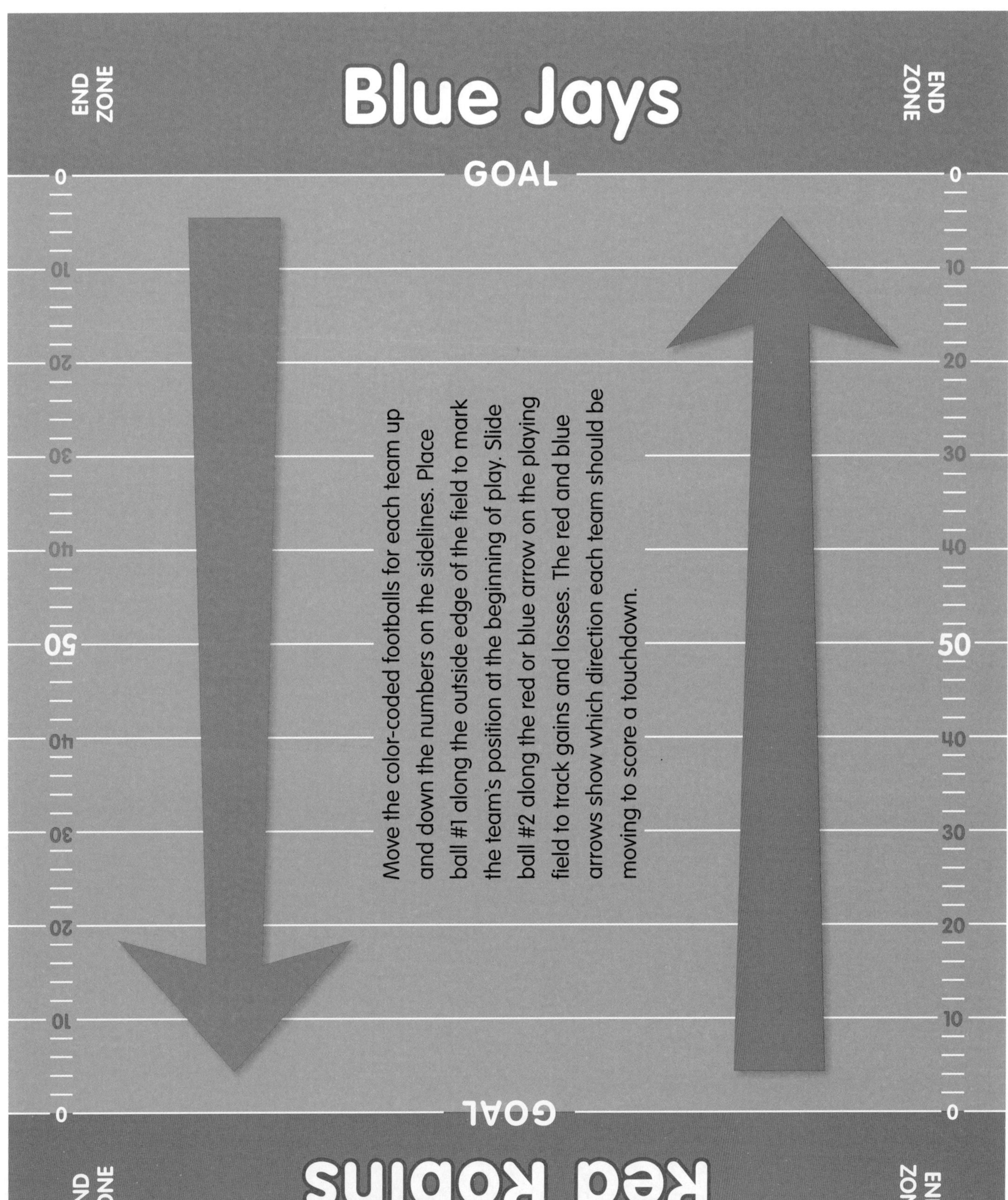

END ZONE
Blue Jays
END ZONE
GOAL
Move the color-coded footballs for each team up and down the numbers on the sidelines. Place ball #1 along the outside edge of the field to mark the team's position at the beginning of play. Slide ball #2 along the red or blue arrow on the playing field to track gains and losses. The red and blue arrows show which direction each team should be moving to score a touchdown.
GOAL
END ZONE
Red Robins
END ZONE

Temperature 1

Juan woke up at 7:30 a.m. and looked at the thermometer. The temperature was 42°F. By noon, it was 18 degrees warmer. What was the temperature at noon?

Temperature 

At lunchtime on the 4th of July, the temperature in Lakeville, Minnesota, hit a record 112°F! When the fireworks began that evening, it was still 99°F. How much had the temperature dropped since lunchtime?

Temperature 

Roshan had to decide what to pack for his trip to Arizona. He looked up the predicted high temperatures for the eight-day trip and saw that they were expected to increase a total of 40 degrees from the first day to the last. The predicted high for the first day was 73°F. What was it for the last day? What was the average temperature increase per day?

Temperature 

Sara ran a marathon last weekend. When the race started, the temperature was 10°C. When Sara reached the halfway point, it was 17 degrees warmer. When she finished the race, the temperature was 14°C. How many degrees did the temperature drop between the halfway point and the end of the race?

Temperature 

Zack has to walk his dog before and after school every day. One day, the temperature was a frigid –16°F in the morning. It had warmed up 11 degrees by the end of the school day, but the windchill factor made it feel 10 degrees colder. How cold did it feel when Zack walked his dog after school?

Temperature 

Jessie went skiing on Saturday. Throughout the day, the temperature changed dramatically. It increased 21 degrees between 8:00 a.m. and noon and then decreased 22 degrees by 6:00 p.m. If the temperature at 6:00 p.m. was –8°C, what was the temperature at 8:00 a.m.?

Temperature 

Marcus kept track of midday temperatures during a full week of school. On Monday, the temperature was 68°F. On Tuesday, it was 9 degrees higher. On Wednesday, it increased 5 more degrees. On Thursday, it was 11 degrees colder than on Wednesday. On Friday, it dropped 6 more degrees. What was the midday temperature on Friday?

Temperature 

While listening to the evening news, Melissa heard the weather forecaster say that the highest temperature that day had been 0°C. When she went to bed at 9:30 p.m., Melissa noticed that the window thermometer in the kitchen showed 28°F. Did the temperature increase or decrease from the reported daytime high, and by how much?

Integers

EMC 3076

© Evan-Moor Corp.

Integers

EMC 3076

© Evan-Moor Corp.

Integers

EMC 3076

© Evan-Moor Corp.

Integers

EMC 3076

© Evan-Moor Corp.

Integers

EMC 3076

© Evan-Moor Corp.

Integers

EMC 3076

© Evan-Moor Corp.

Integers

EMC 3076

© Evan-Moor Corp.

Integers

EMC 3076

© Evan-Moor Corp.

Temperature 9

Sasha did a report on extreme temperatures in Alaska. In Juneau one day, a temperature of –9°C dropped 23 degrees in two hours. The same day, the temperature in Fairbanks dropped 19 degrees in two hours to a bone-chilling –30°F. Which city was colder after the temperature dropped?

Temperature 10

During her vacation in Florida, Lily swam every day in the Gulf of Mexico. On the first day, the water temperature was 85°F. It rose 3 degrees the second day, dropped 7 degrees the third day, and went up 5 degrees the fourth day. On the fifth day, it was 87°F. Did it increase or decrease from the fourth day to the fifth day? On which day was the water the warmest?

Football 1

The Blue Jays and the Red Robins are battling for the middle school football championship. The Robins kick off, and the Jays get the ball at their own 20-yard line. They gain 15 yards on the first play, but lose 3 on the next and lose 8 more after that. They finally gain back 9 yards. How many total yards did the Blue Jays gain or lose?

Football 2

Now the Blue Jays kick to the Robins. The Robins catch the ball at their 38-yard line and run 37 yards before being tackled. In the next three plays, they lose a total of 12 yards. At what yard line do they end up?

Football 3

The Robins try kicking a field goal but miss it. Now the Jays get the ball again. They try a running play but end up losing 15 yards. They gain back 3 yards on the second down. Then they gain 7 more. They go for first and ten on the fourth down but lose 2 yards instead. How many total yards did the Jays gain or lose?

Football 4

Taking over at the Jays' 30-yard line, the Robins throw a 23-yard pass! On the next play, they gain 3 yards running, but on second and goal, a short pass to the end zone is intercepted by a Blue Jay! The Jay runs 42 yards down the field before being tackled! At what yard line was the Blue Jay stopped?

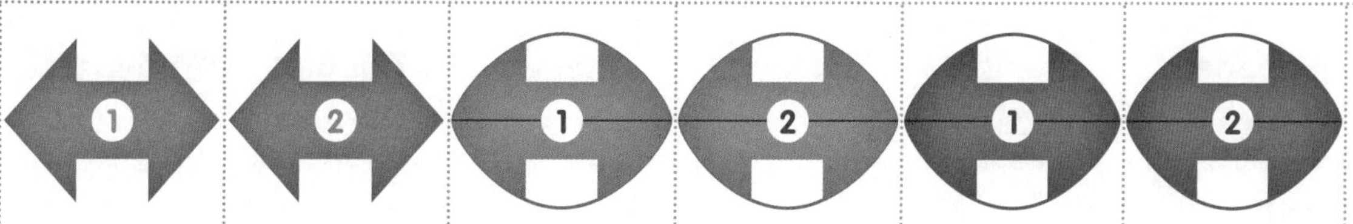

Integers
EMC 3076

Integers
EMC 3076

Integers
EMC 3076

Integers
EMC 3076

Integers
EMC 3076

Integers
EMC 3076

Integers
EMC 3076

Integers
EMC 3076

Integers
EMC 3076

Integers
EMC 3076

Integers
EMC 3076

Integers
EMC 3076

Football 5

A 10-yard gain on the next play puts the Jays at the Robins' 44-yard line. They gain 7 yards more on each of the next two plays. Then they gain 9 more, but a penalty is called and the ball is moved back 15 yards. How many total yards did the Blue Jays gain or lose in the last three plays?

Football 6

In the two minutes left before halftime, the Blue Jays throw two incomplete passes before completing a short pass that gains them only 9 yards. A penalty against the Robins on that play gives the Jays 5 more yards and a first down at the 22-yard line. At what yard line were the Blue Jays at the beginning of the play?

Football 7

The second half of the game starts with the score still zero to zero. Now the Jays kick off to the Robins. The Robins catch the ball at their 18-yard line. In the next three plays, they gain 7 yards, lose 12 yards, and gain 27 yards. At what yard line did each of the plays end?

Football 8

On the next play, a Red Robin catches a pass at the 50-yard line and runs the ball 3 yards before he trips and fumbles. The ball bounces backward 4 yards. Then a Blue Jay picks it up and runs 16 yards downfield before he's tackled. At what yard line was he tackled?

Football 9

After three incomplete passes, the Blue Jays unsuccessfully attempt a field goal and the Robins get the ball. They lose 9 yards on the first play and 11 on the second. Then they complete an amazing 42-yard pass! How many more yards do the Robins need to gain to score a touchdown?

Football 10

The Robins call a time out, but they take too long and lose 10 yards for delay of game. They complete a pass on the next play for a 23-yard gain but then lose 8 yards and gain back only 6. On the next play, the Jays intercept a pass at their own 10-yard line. They run the ball all the way down the field for a touchdown to win the game! How many yards was the Robins' pass, and how many yards was the touchdown run?

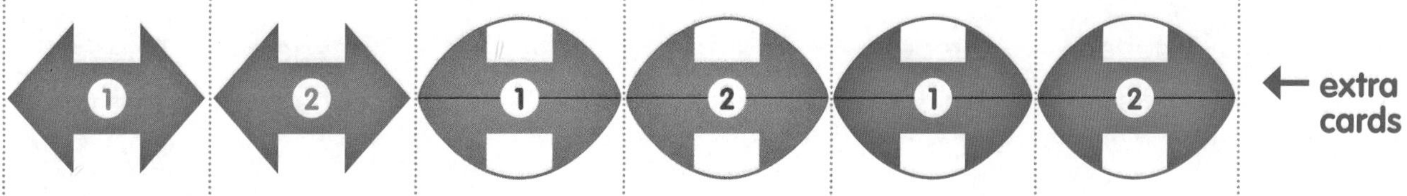

← extra cards

Integers

EMC 3076

© Evan-Moor Corp.

Integers

EMC 3076

© Evan-Moor Corp.

Integers

EMC 3076

© Evan-Moor Corp.

Integers

EMC 3076

© Evan-Moor Corp.

Integers

EMC 3076

© Evan-Moor Corp.

Integers

EMC 3076

© Evan-Moor Corp.

Integers

EMC 3076

© Evan-Moor Corp.

Integers

EMC 3076

© Evan-Moor Corp.

Integers

EMC 3076

© Evan-Moor Corp.

Integers

EMC 3076

© Evan-Moor Corp.

Integers

EMC 3076

© Evan-Moor Corp.

Integers

EMC 3076

© Evan-Moor Corp.

Take It to Your Seat Centers

Multi-Digit Division

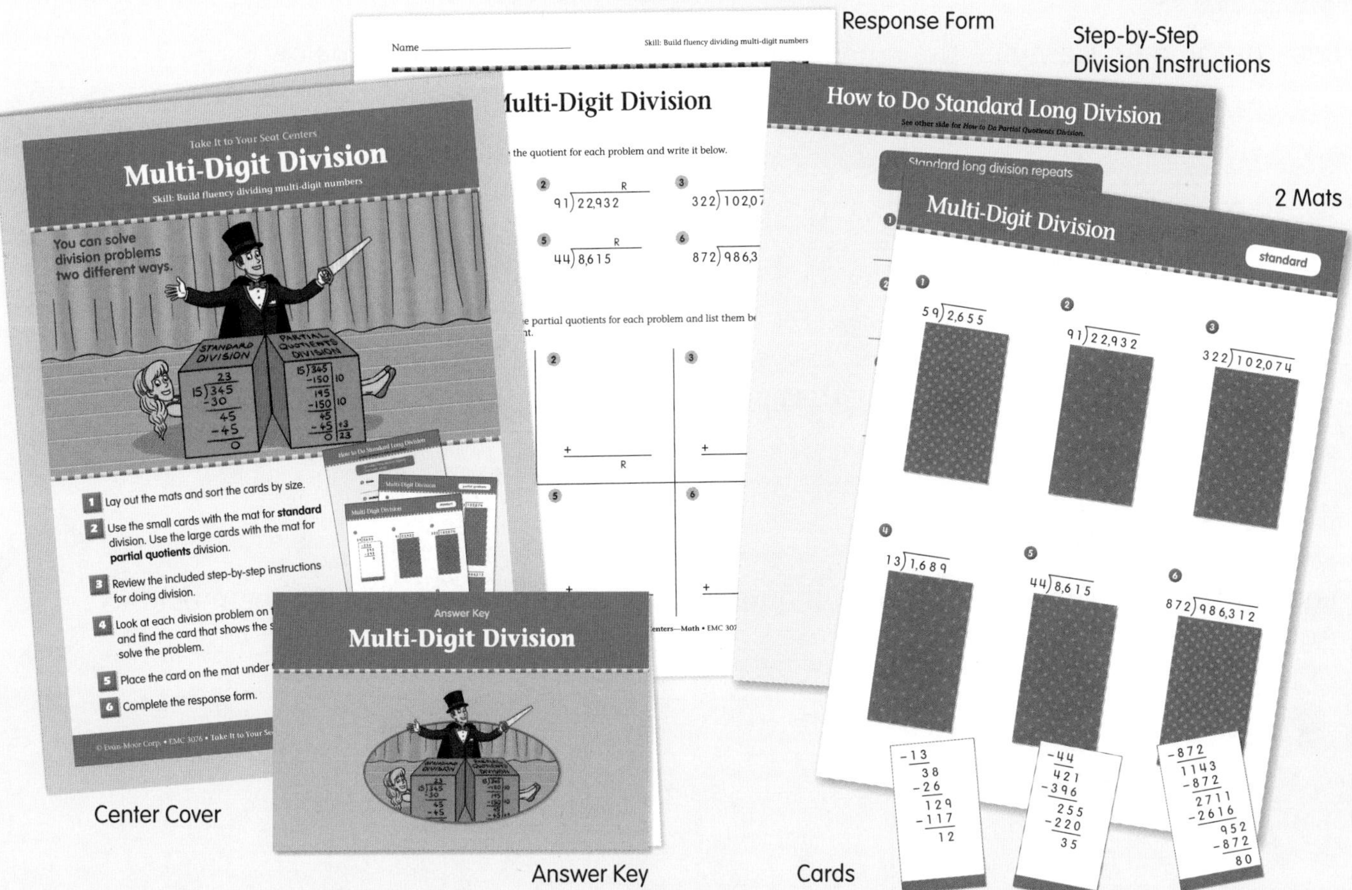

Skill: Build fluency dividing multi-digit numbers

Steps to Follow

1. **Prepare the center.** (See page 3.)
2. **Introduce the center.** State the goal. Say: *You will solve multi-digit division problems, using standard long division or partial quotients division or both.*
3. **Teach the skill.** Demonstrate how to use the center with individual students or small groups.
4. **Practice the skill.** Have students use the center independently or with a partner.

Contents

Name ______________________ Skill: Build fluency dividing multi-digit numbers

Multi-Digit Division

Standard

Look at the mat. Compute the quotient for each problem and write it below.

1. 59)2,655 — 45 R 0
2. 91)22,932 — R
3. 322)102,074 — R
4. 13)1,689 — R
5. 44)8,615 — R
6. 872)986,312 — R

Partial Quotients

Look at the mat. Compute the partial quotients for each problem and list them below. Add to show the final quotient.

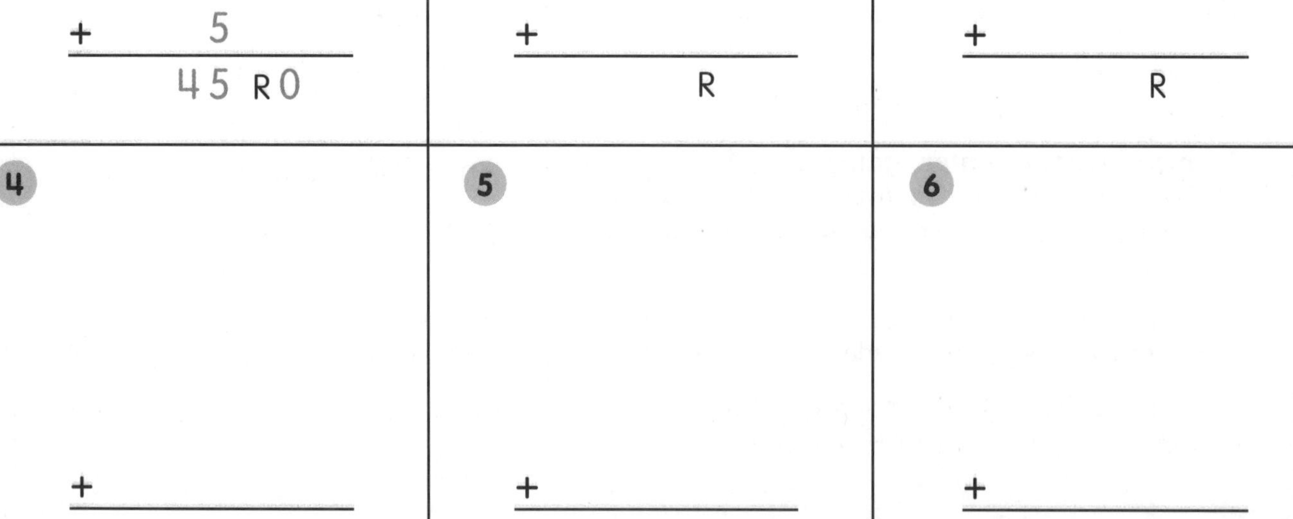

1.
10
10
10
10
\+ 5
45 R0

2. \+ ____ R

3. \+ ____ R

4. \+ ____ R

5. \+ ____ R

6. \+ ____ R

Multi-Digit Division

Skill: Build fluency dividing multi-digit numbers

You can solve division problems two different ways.

STANDARD DIVISION

```
     23
15)345
  -30
   45
  -45
    0
```

PARTIAL QUOTIENTS DIVISION

```
15)345
  -150 | 10
   195 |
  -150 | 10
    45 |
  - 45 | +3
     0 | 23
```

1. Lay out the mats and sort the cards by size.
2. Use the small cards with the mat for **standard** division. Use the large cards with the mat for **partial quotients** division.
3. Review the included step-by-step instructions for doing division.
4. Look at each division problem on the mats and find the card that shows the steps to solve the problem.
5. Place the card on the mat under the problem.
6. Complete the response form.

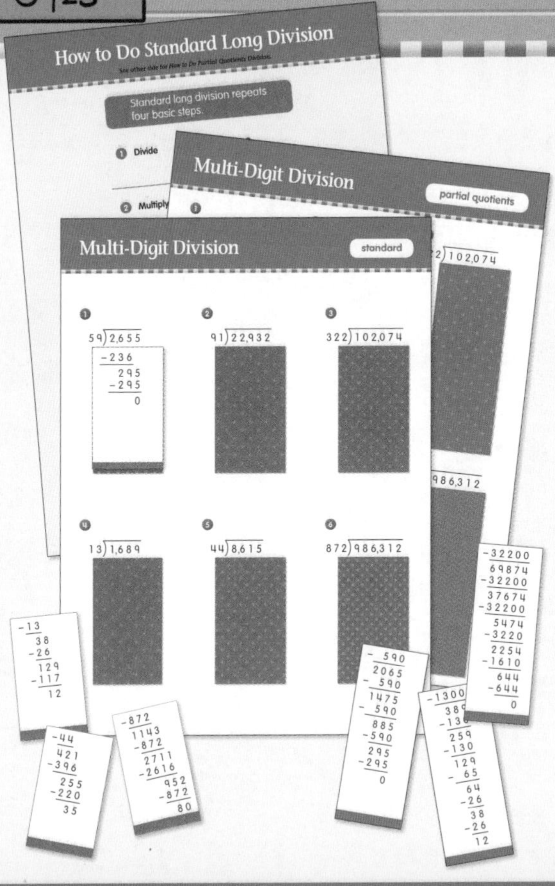

Multi-Digit Division

Answer Key

(fold)

Response Form

Multi-Digit Division

Standard

Look at the mat. Compute the quotient for each problem and write it below.

1. 59)2,655 = 45 R 0
2. 91)22,932 = 252 R 0
3. 322)102,074 = 317 R 0
4. 13)1,689 = 129 R 12
5. 44)8,615 = 195 R 35
6. 872)986,312 = 1,131 R 80

Partial Quotients

Look at the mat. Compute the partial quotients for each problem and list them below. Add to show the final quotient.

1	2	3
10 10 10 10 + 5 45 R 0	100 100 20 20 10 + 2 252 R 0	100 100 100 10 5 + 2 317 R 0

4	5	6
100 10 10 5 2 + 2 129 R 12	100 50 25 10 + 10 195 R 35	1,000 100 10 10 10 + 1 1,131 R 80

Answer Key

Multi-Digit Division

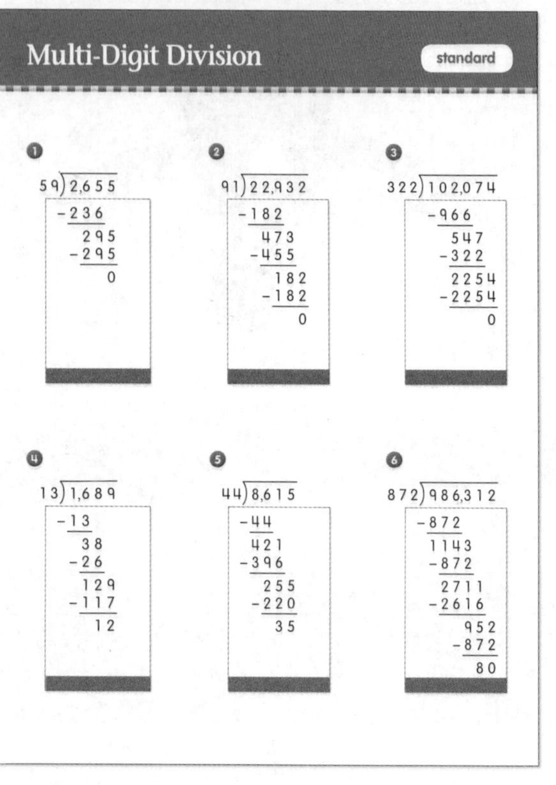

Multi-Digit Division — standard

1 59)2,655

```
 -236
   295
  -295
     0
```

2 91)22,932

```
 -182
   473
  -455
    182
   -182
      0
```

3 322)102,074

```
 -966
   547
  -322
   2254
  -2254
      0
```

4 13)1,689

```
 -13
   38
  -26
   129
  -117
    12
```

5 44)8,615

```
 -44
  421
 -396
   255
  -220
    35
```

6 872)986,312

```
 -872
  1143
  -872
   2711
  -2616
     952
    -872
      80
```

Multi-Digit Division — partial quotients

1 59)2,655

```
 -  590
   2065
 -  590
   1475
 -  590
    885
   -590
    295
   -295
      0
```

2 91)22,932

```
 -  9100
   13832
 -  9100
    4732
   -1820
    2912
   -1820
    1092
 -   910
     182
    -182
       0
```

3 322)102,074

```
 -32200
  69874
 -32200
  37674
 -32200
   5474
  -3220
   2254
  -1610
    644
   -644
      0
```

4 13)1,689

```
 -1300
   389
  -130
   259
  -130
   129
 -  65
    64
   -26
    38
   -26
    12
```

5 44)8,615

```
 -4400
  4215
 -2200
  2015
 -1100
   915
  -440
   475
  -440
    35
```

6 872)986,312

```
 -872000
  114312
 - 87200
   27112
 -  8720
   18392
 -  8720
    9672
   -8720
     952
    -872
      80
```

How to Do Standard Long Division

See other side for *How to Do Partial Quotients Division*.

Standard long division repeats four basic steps.

1 Divide

```
       3
123)4,567
```

2 Multiply

123 × 3 = **369**

```
       3
123)4,567
     369
```

3 Subtract

```
       3
123)4,567
    -369
      87
```

4 Bring down

```
       3
123)4,567
    -369↓
      877
```

Repeat the steps until there is no remainder or until the remainder is smaller than the divisor.

```
      quotient
      37 R16
123)4,567
    -369
      877
     -861
       16
```

How to Do Partial Quotients Division

See other side for *How to Do Standard Long Division*.

Partial quotients division finds a partial answer at each step. The partial answers are added together to find the final quotient.

1 Use mental math to multiply the divisor by a number (factor) that will give you the biggest product possible but still be less than the dividend. (Using multiples of 10 or doubling the divisor usually works well.)

$$123\overline{)4{,}567}$$

$$\begin{array}{r} 123 \\ \times\ 10 \\ \hline 1{,}230 \end{array}$$

2 List the factors in a column next to the division. (You will add up the factors later.)

$$\begin{array}{r|l} 123\overline{)4{,}567} & \\ & 10 \end{array}$$

3 Each time you multiply, write the product under the dividend and subtract.

$$\begin{array}{r|l} 123\overline{)4{,}567} & \\ -1230 & 10 \\ \hline 3337 & \end{array}$$

4 Repeat steps 1, 2, and 3 until there is no remainder or until the remainder is smaller than the divisor.

$$\begin{array}{r|l} 123\overline{)4{,}567} & \\ -1230 & 10 \\ \hline 3337 & \\ -2460 & 20 \\ \hline 877 & \\ -615 & 5 \\ \hline 262 & \\ -246 & 2 \\ \hline 16 & \end{array}$$

5 Add the list of factors (see step 2) to get the final quotient.

$$\begin{array}{r|r} 123\overline{)4{,}567} & \\ -1230 & 10 \\ \hline 3337 & \\ -2460 & 20 \\ \hline 877 & \\ -615 & 5 \\ \hline 262 & \\ -246 & +\ 2 \\ \hline 16 & 37 \end{array}$$

quotient

37 R16

Multi-Digit Division

standard

1

$59\overline{)2{,}655}$

2

$91\overline{)22{,}932}$

3

$322\overline{)102{,}074}$

4

$13\overline{)1{,}689}$

5

$44\overline{)8{,}615}$

6

$872\overline{)986{,}312}$

Multi-Digit Division

partial quotients

59)2,655

91)22,932

3

322)102,074

4

13)1,689

44)8,615

872)986,312

−236	−182	−966	−13	−44	−872
295	473	547	38	421	1143
−295	−455	−322	−26	−396	−872
0	182	2254	129	255	2711
	−182	−2254	−117	−220	−2616
	0	0	12	35	952
					−872
					80

− 590	− 9100	−32200	−1300	−4400	−872000
2065	13832	69874	389	4215	114312
− 590	− 9100	−32200	−130	−2200	− 87200
1475	4732	37674	259	2015	27112
− 590	−1820	−32200	−130	−1100	− 8720
885	2912	5474	129	915	18392
−590	−1820	−3220	− 65	−440	− 8720
295	1092	2254	64	475	9672
−295	− 910	−1610	−26	−440	−8720
0	182	644	38	35	952
	−182	−644	−26		−872
	0	0	12		80

Multi-Digit Division
EMC 3076
© Evan-Moor Corp.

Multi-Digit Division
EMC 3076
© Evan-Moor Corp.

Multi-Digit Division
EMC 3076
© Evan-Moor Corp.

Multi-Digit Division
EMC 3076
© Evan-Moor Corp.

Multi-Digit Division
EMC 3076
© Evan-Moor Corp.

Multi-Digit Division
EMC 3076
© Evan-Moor Corp.

Multi-Digit Division
EMC 3076
© Evan-Moor Corp.

Multi-Digit Division
EMC 3076
© Evan-Moor Corp.

Multi-Digit Division
EMC 3076
© Evan-Moor Corp.

Multi-Digit Division
EMC 3076
© Evan-Moor Corp.

Take It to Your Seat Centers

Dividing with Decimals

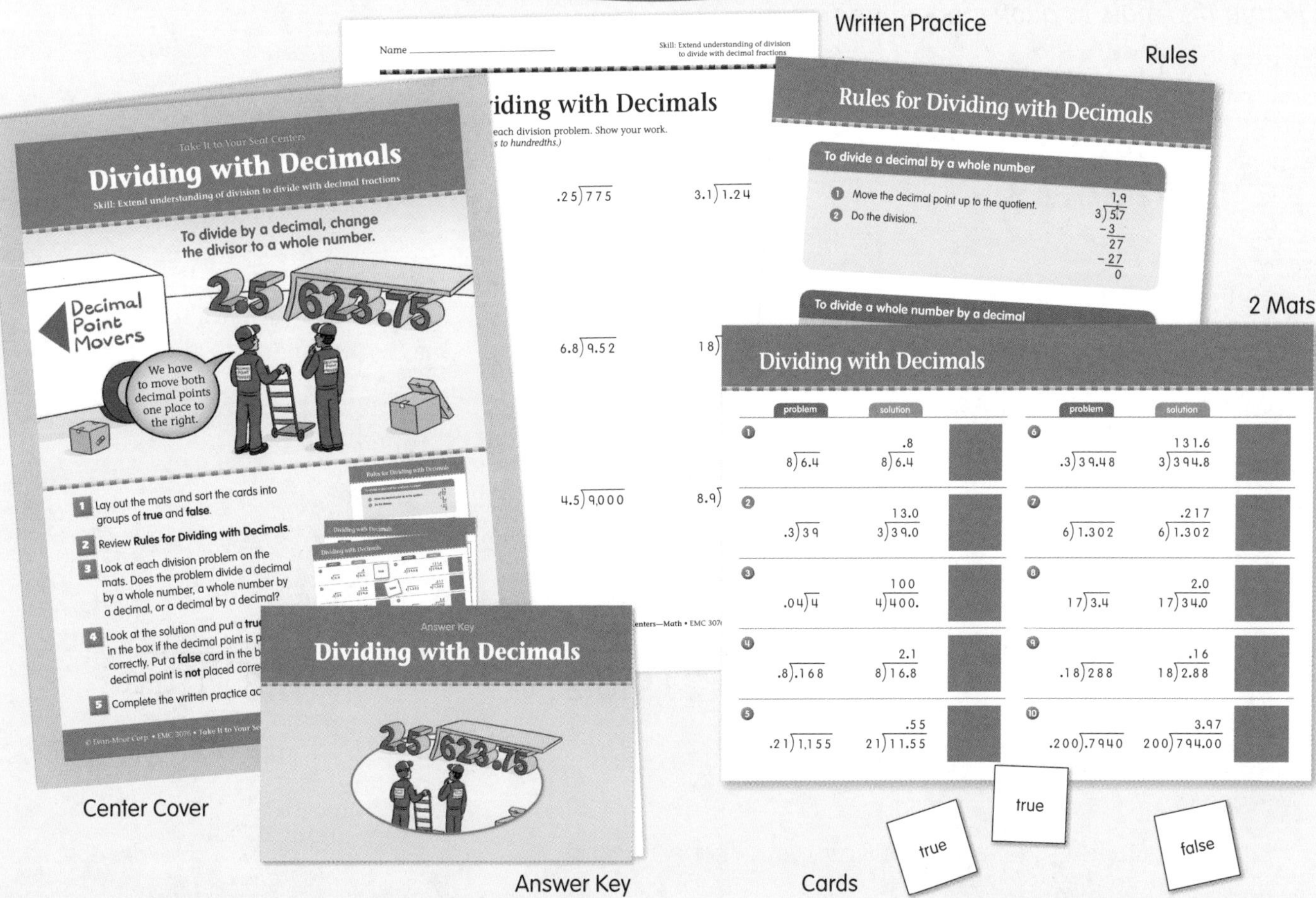

Skill: Extend understanding of division to divide with decimal fractions

Steps to Follow

1. **Prepare the center.** (See page 3.)
2. **Introduce the center.** State the goal. Say: *You will look at the division problems and solutions on the mats and decide whether the decimal points in the solutions have been moved correctly.*
3. **Teach the skill.** Demonstrate how to use the center with individual students or small groups.
4. **Practice the skill.** Have students use the center independently or with a partner.

Contents

Name ____________________

Skill: Extend understanding of division to divide with decimal fractions

Dividing with Decimals

Compute the quotient for each division problem. Show your work.
(Round decimals in quotients to hundredths.)

$9\overline{)56.79}$

$.25\overline{)775}$

$3.1\overline{)1.24}$

$7.7\overline{)108}$

$6.8\overline{)9.52}$

$18\overline{)1.44}$

$1.62\overline{).00486}$

$4.5\overline{)9{,}000}$

$8.9\overline{)5.17}$

Dividing with Decimals

Skill: Extend understanding of division to divide with decimal fractions

To divide by a decimal, change the divisor to a whole number.

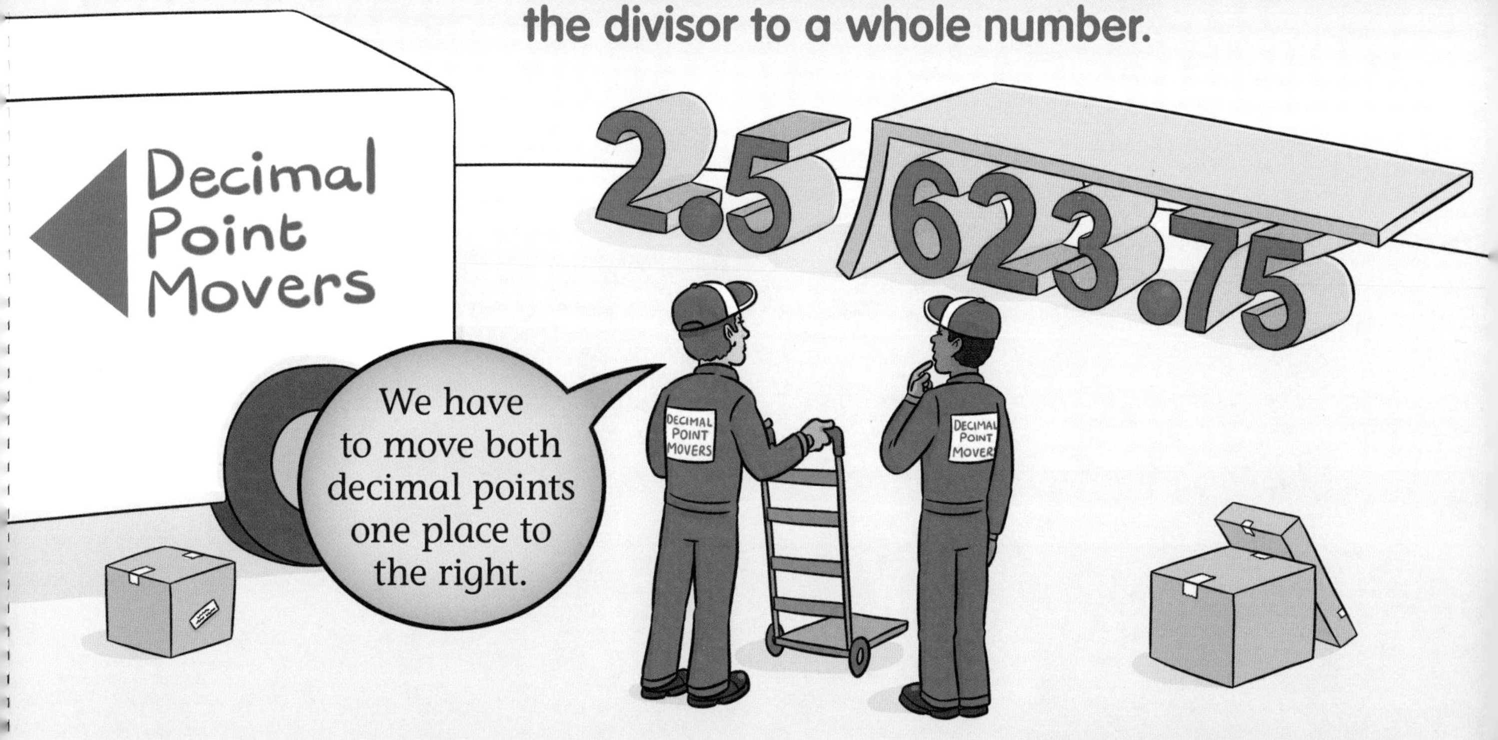

Decimal Point Movers

2.5)623.75

We have to move both decimal points one place to the right.

1. Lay out the mats and sort the cards into groups of **true** and **false**.
2. Review **Rules for Dividing with Decimals**.
3. Look at each division problem on the mats. Does the problem divide a decimal by a whole number, a whole number by a decimal, or a decimal by a decimal?
4. Look at the solution and put a **true** card in the box if the decimal point is placed correctly. Put a **false** card in the box if the decimal point is **not** placed correctly.
5. Complete the written practice activity.

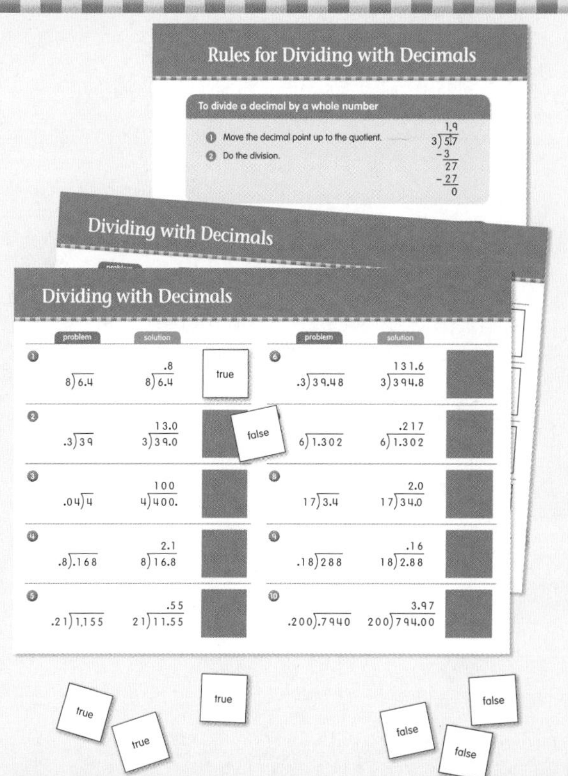

Dividing with Decimals

Answer Key

(fold)

Written Practice

Dividing with Decimals

Compute the quotient for each division problem. Show your work.
(Round decimals in quotients to hundredths.)

$9\overline{)56.79}$ = 6.31	$.25\overline{)775.00}$ = 3,100	$3.1\overline{)1.24}$ = .4
$7.7\overline{)108.00}$ = 14.03	$6.8\overline{)9.52}$ = 1.4	$18\overline{)1.44}$ = .08
$1.62\overline{).00486}$ = .003	$4.5\overline{)9{,}000.0}$ = 2,000	$8.9\overline{)5.17}$ = .58

Answer Key

Dividing with Decimals

Dividing with Decimals

#	problem	solution	
1	$8\overline{)6.4}$	$\begin{array}{r}.8\\8\overline{)6.4}\end{array}$	true
2	$.3\overline{)39}$	$\begin{array}{r}13.0\\3\overline{)39.0}\end{array}$	false
3	$.04\overline{)4}$	$\begin{array}{r}100\\4\overline{)400.}\end{array}$	true
4	$.8\overline{).168}$	$\begin{array}{r}2.1\\8\overline{)16.8}\end{array}$	false
5	$.21\overline{)1{,}155}$	$\begin{array}{r}.55\\21\overline{)11.55}\end{array}$	false

#	problem	solution	
6	$.3\overline{)39.48}$	$\begin{array}{r}131.6\\3\overline{)394.8}\end{array}$	true
7	$6\overline{)1.302}$	$\begin{array}{r}.217\\6\overline{)1.302}\end{array}$	true
8	$17\overline{)3.4}$	$\begin{array}{r}2.0\\17\overline{)34.0}\end{array}$	false
9	$.18\overline{)288}$	$\begin{array}{r}.16\\18\overline{)2.88}\end{array}$	false
10	$.200\overline{).7940}$	$\begin{array}{r}3.97\\200\overline{)794.00}\end{array}$	true

Dividing with Decimals

#	problem	solution	
11	$5\overline{).01515}$	$\begin{array}{r}.0303\\5\overline{)0.1515}\end{array}$	false
12	$1.71\overline{).342}$	$\begin{array}{r}.2\\171\overline{)34.2}\end{array}$	true
13	$11\overline{)3.96}$	$\begin{array}{r}.36\\11\overline{)3.96}\end{array}$	true
14	$6.4\overline{)2.56}$	$\begin{array}{r}.04\\64\overline{)2.56}\end{array}$	false
15	$1.06\overline{)212}$	$\begin{array}{r}200\\106\overline{)21200.}\end{array}$	true

#	problem	solution	
16	$.68\overline{)4{,}148}$	$\begin{array}{r}6{,}100\\68\overline{)414{,}800.}\end{array}$	true
17	$5.1\overline{)1.53}$	$\begin{array}{r}.003\\51\overline{).153}\end{array}$	false
18	$.567\overline{)1{,}134}$	$\begin{array}{r}.2\\567\overline{)113.4}\end{array}$	false
19	$28\overline{)4.20}$	$\begin{array}{r}.15\\28\overline{)4.20}\end{array}$	true
20	$71.9\overline{)3{,}738.8}$	$\begin{array}{r}.52\\719\overline{)373.88}\end{array}$	false

Rules for Dividing with Decimals

To divide a decimal by a whole number

1. Move the decimal point up to the quotient.
2. Do the division.

$$\begin{array}{r} 1.9 \\ 3\overline{)5.7} \\ -3 \\ \hline 27 \\ -27 \\ \hline 0 \end{array}$$

To divide a whole number by a decimal

1. Move the decimal point in the divisor to create a whole number.
2. Add a decimal point at the end of the dividend and move it the same number of places to the right as you moved the decimal point in the divisor. (Add zeros to create the number of places you need to move the decimal point.)
3. Do the division.

$$\begin{array}{r} 120 \\ .7\overline{)84.0.} \\ -7 \\ \hline 14 \\ -14 \\ \hline 00 \\ -00 \\ \hline 0 \end{array}$$

To divide a decimal by a decimal

1. Move the decimal point in the divisor to create a whole number.
2. Move the decimal point in the dividend the same number of places to the right. (Add zeros, if necessary, to create the number of places you need to move the decimal point.)
3. Do the division.

$$\begin{array}{r} 140 \\ .14\overline{)19.60.} \\ -14 \\ \hline 56 \\ -56 \\ \hline 00 \\ -00 \\ \hline 0 \end{array}$$

Dividing with Decimals

#	problem	solution
1	$8\overline{)6.4}$	$8\overline{)6.4}$ = .8
2	$.3\overline{)39}$	$3\overline{)39.0}$ = 13.0
3	$.04\overline{)4}$	$4\overline{)400.}$ = 100
4	$.8\overline{).168}$	$8\overline{)16.8}$ = 2.1
5	$.21\overline{)1{,}155}$	$21\overline{)11.55}$ = .55
6	$.3\overline{)39.48}$	$3\overline{)394.8}$ = 131.6
7	$6\overline{)1.302}$	$6\overline{)1.302}$ = .217
8	$17\overline{)3.4}$	$17\overline{)34.0}$ = 2.0
9	$.18\overline{)288}$	$18\overline{)2.88}$ = .16
10	$.200\overline{).7940}$	$200\overline{)794.00}$ = 3.97

Dividing with Decimals

#	problem	solution
11	$5\overline{).01515}$	$\begin{array}{r} .0303 \\ 5\overline{)0.1515} \end{array}$
12	$1.71\overline{).342}$	$\begin{array}{r} .2 \\ 171\overline{)34.2} \end{array}$
13	$11\overline{)3.96}$	$\begin{array}{r} .36 \\ 11\overline{)3.96} \end{array}$
14	$6.4\overline{)2.56}$	$\begin{array}{r} .04 \\ 64\overline{)2.56} \end{array}$
15	$1.06\overline{)212}$	$\begin{array}{r} 200 \\ 106\overline{)21200.} \end{array}$
16	$.68\overline{)4{,}148}$	$\begin{array}{r} 6{,}100 \\ 68\overline{)414{,}800.} \end{array}$
17	$5.1\overline{)1.53}$	$\begin{array}{r} .003 \\ 51\overline{).153} \end{array}$
18	$.567\overline{)1{,}134}$	$\begin{array}{r} .2 \\ 567\overline{)113.4} \end{array}$
19	$28\overline{)4.20}$	$\begin{array}{r} .15 \\ 28\overline{)4.20} \end{array}$
20	$71.9\overline{)3{,}738.8}$	$\begin{array}{r} .52 \\ 719\overline{)373.88} \end{array}$

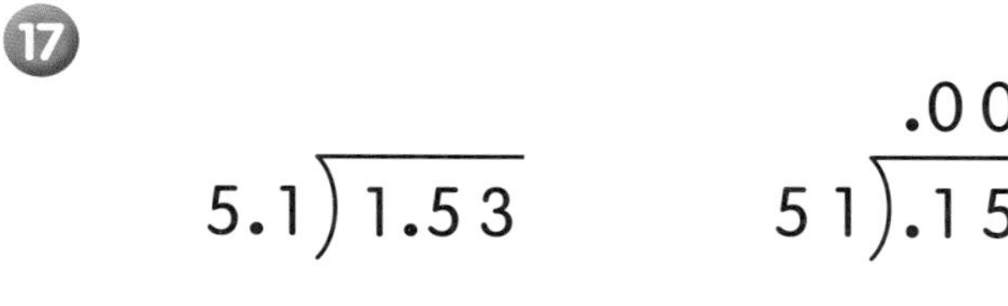

true	true	true	true	true
true	true	true	true	true
true	true	true	true	true
true	true	true	true	true
false	false	false	false	false
false	false	false	false	false
false	false	false	false	false
false	false	false	false	false

Dividing with Decimals EMC 3076 © Evan-Moor Corp.	Dividing with Decimals EMC 3076 © Evan-Moor Corp.	Dividing with Decimals EMC 3076 © Evan-Moor Corp.	Dividing with Decimals EMC 3076 © Evan-Moor Corp.	Dividing with Decimals EMC 3076 © Evan-Moor Corp.
Dividing with Decimals EMC 3076 © Evan-Moor Corp.	Dividing with Decimals EMC 3076 © Evan-Moor Corp.	Dividing with Decimals EMC 3076 © Evan-Moor Corp.	Dividing with Decimals EMC 3076 © Evan-Moor Corp.	Dividing with Decimals EMC 3076 © Evan-Moor Corp.
Dividing with Decimals EMC 3076 © Evan-Moor Corp.	Dividing with Decimals EMC 3076 © Evan-Moor Corp.	Dividing with Decimals EMC 3076 © Evan-Moor Corp.	Dividing with Decimals EMC 3076 © Evan-Moor Corp.	Dividing with Decimals EMC 3076 © Evan-Moor Corp.
Dividing with Decimals EMC 3076 © Evan-Moor Corp.	Dividing with Decimals EMC 3076 © Evan-Moor Corp.	Dividing with Decimals EMC 3076 © Evan-Moor Corp.	Dividing with Decimals EMC 3076 © Evan-Moor Corp.	Dividing with Decimals EMC 3076 © Evan-Moor Corp.
Dividing with Decimals EMC 3076 © Evan-Moor Corp.	Dividing with Decimals EMC 3076 © Evan-Moor Corp.	Dividing with Decimals EMC 3076 © Evan-Moor Corp.	Dividing with Decimals EMC 3076 © Evan-Moor Corp.	Dividing with Decimals EMC 3076 © Evan-Moor Corp.
Dividing with Decimals EMC 3076 © Evan-Moor Corp.	Dividing with Decimals EMC 3076 © Evan-Moor Corp.	Dividing with Decimals EMC 3076 © Evan-Moor Corp.	Dividing with Decimals EMC 3076 © Evan-Moor Corp.	Dividing with Decimals EMC 3076 © Evan-Moor Corp.
Dividing with Decimals EMC 3076 © Evan-Moor Corp.	Dividing with Decimals EMC 3076 © Evan-Moor Corp.	Dividing with Decimals EMC 3076 © Evan-Moor Corp.	Dividing with Decimals EMC 3076 © Evan-Moor Corp.	Dividing with Decimals EMC 3076 © Evan-Moor Corp.
Dividing with Decimals EMC 3076 © Evan-Moor Corp.	Dividing with Decimals EMC 3076 © Evan-Moor Corp.	Dividing with Decimals EMC 3076 © Evan-Moor Corp.	Dividing with Decimals EMC 3076 © Evan-Moor Corp.	Dividing with Decimals EMC 3076 © Evan-Moor Corp.

Take It to Your Seat Centers

Dividing Fractions

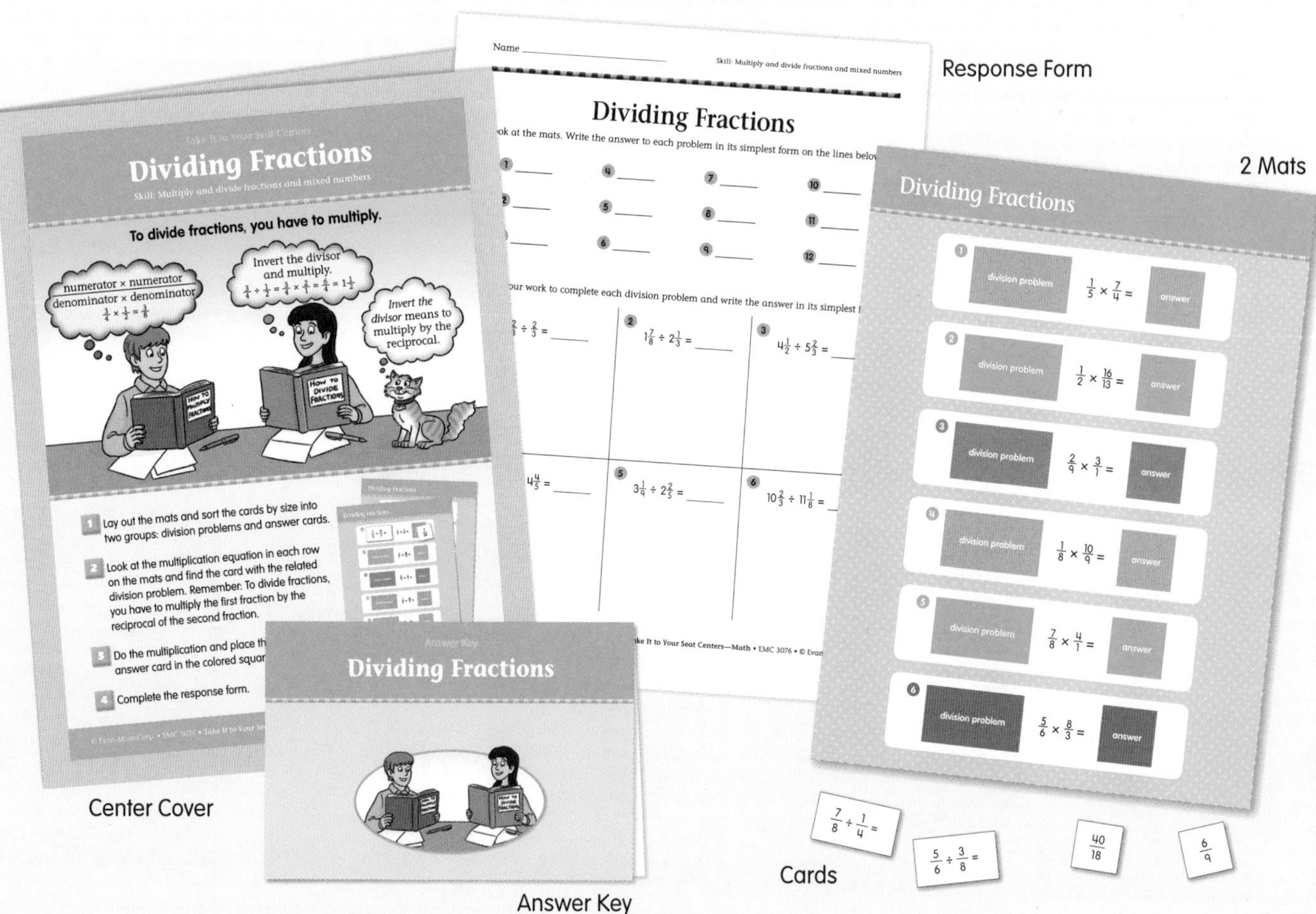

Skill: Multiply and divide fractions and mixed numbers

Steps to Follow

1. **Prepare the center.** (See page 3.)
2. **Introduce the center.** State the goal. Say: *You will find the division problem that goes with each multiplication equation on the mats and then compute the answer.*
3. **Teach the skill.** Demonstrate how to use the center with individual students or small groups.
4. **Practice the skill.** Have students use the center independently or with a partner.

Contents

Name ______________________ Skill: Multiply and divide fractions and mixed numbers

Dividing Fractions

Look at the mats. Write the answer to each problem in its simplest form on the lines below.

1 ______ 4 ______ 7 ______ 10 ______

2 ______ 5 ______ 8 ______ 11 ______

3 ______ 6 ______ 9 ______ 12 ______

Show your work to complete each division problem and write the answer in its simplest form.

1 $\frac{2}{3} \div \frac{2}{3} =$ ______	2 $1\frac{7}{8} \div 2\frac{1}{3} =$ ______	3 $4\frac{1}{2} \div 5\frac{2}{3} =$ ______
4 $2\frac{1}{2} \div 4\frac{4}{5} =$ ______	5 $3\frac{1}{9} \div 2\frac{2}{5} =$ ______	6 $10\frac{2}{3} \div 11\frac{1}{8} =$ ______

Dividing Fractions

Skill: Multiply and divide fractions and mixed numbers

To divide fractions, you have to multiply.

1. Lay out the mats and sort the cards by size into two groups: division problems and answer cards.
2. Look at the multiplication equation in each row on the mats and find the card with the related division problem. Remember: To divide fractions, you have to multiply the first fraction by the reciprocal of the second fraction.
3. Do the multiplication and place the correct answer card in the colored square.
4. Complete the response form.

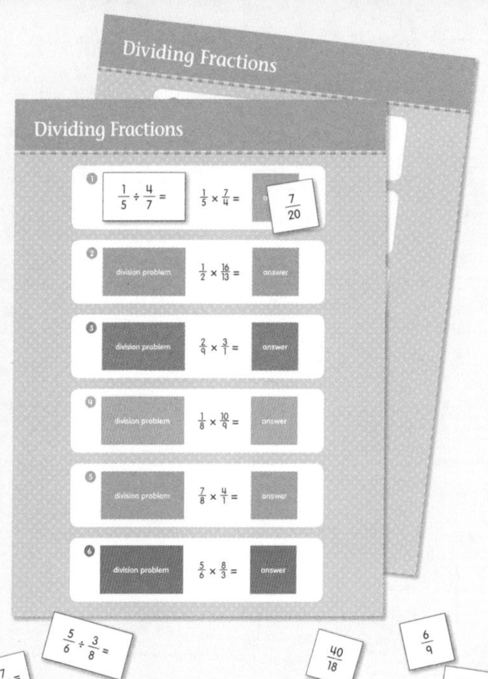

Answer Key

Dividing Fractions

(fold)

Response Form

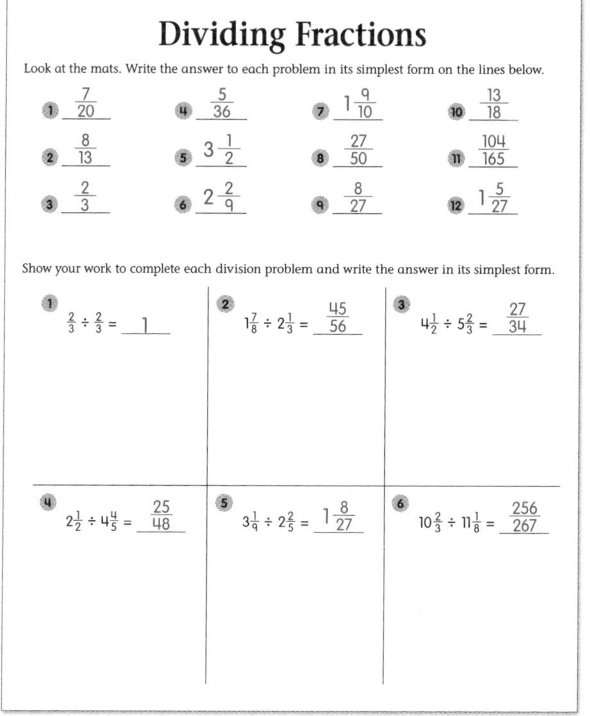

Dividing Fractions

Look at the mats. Write the answer to each problem in its simplest form on the lines below.

1 $\frac{7}{20}$	4 $\frac{5}{36}$	7 $1\frac{9}{10}$	10 $\frac{13}{18}$
2 $\frac{8}{13}$	5 $3\frac{1}{2}$	8 $\frac{27}{50}$	11 $\frac{104}{165}$
3 $\frac{2}{3}$	6 $2\frac{2}{9}$	9 $\frac{8}{27}$	12 $1\frac{5}{27}$

Show your work to complete each division problem and write the answer in its simplest form.

1 $\frac{2}{3} \div \frac{2}{3} = 1$	2 $1\frac{7}{8} \div 2\frac{1}{3} = \frac{45}{56}$	3 $4\frac{1}{2} \div 5\frac{2}{3} = \frac{27}{34}$
4 $2\frac{1}{2} \div 4\frac{4}{5} = \frac{25}{48}$	5 $3\frac{1}{9} \div 2\frac{2}{5} = 1\frac{8}{27}$	6 $10\frac{2}{3} \div 11\frac{1}{8} = \frac{256}{267}$

Answer Key

Dividing Fractions

Dividing Fractions

1. $\frac{1}{5} \div \frac{4}{7} =$ $\frac{1}{5} \times \frac{7}{4} =$ $\frac{7}{20}$

2. $\frac{1}{2} \div \frac{13}{16} =$ $\frac{1}{2} \times \frac{16}{13} =$ $\frac{16}{26}$

3. $\frac{2}{9} \div \frac{1}{3} =$ $\frac{2}{9} \times \frac{3}{1} =$ $\frac{6}{9}$

4. $\frac{1}{8} \div \frac{9}{10} =$ $\frac{1}{8} \times \frac{10}{9} =$ $\frac{10}{72}$

5. $\frac{7}{8} \div \frac{1}{4} =$ $\frac{7}{8} \times \frac{4}{1} =$ $\frac{28}{8}$

6. $\frac{5}{6} \div \frac{3}{8} =$ $\frac{5}{6} \times \frac{8}{3} =$ $\frac{40}{18}$

Dividing Fractions

7. $\frac{19}{20} \div \frac{1}{2} =$ $\frac{19}{20} \times \frac{2}{1} =$ $\frac{38}{20}$

8. $1\frac{4}{5} \div 3\frac{1}{3} =$ $\frac{9}{5} \times \frac{3}{10} =$ $\frac{27}{50}$

9. $2\frac{1}{3} \div 7\frac{7}{8} =$ $\frac{7}{3} \times \frac{8}{63} =$ $\frac{56}{189}$

10. $3\frac{1}{4} \div 4\frac{1}{2} =$ $\frac{13}{4} \times \frac{2}{9} =$ $\frac{26}{36}$

11. $5\frac{1}{5} \div 8\frac{1}{4} =$ $\frac{26}{5} \times \frac{4}{33} =$ $\frac{104}{165}$

12. $6\frac{2}{3} \div 5\frac{5}{8} =$ $\frac{20}{3} \times \frac{8}{45} =$ $\frac{160}{135}$

Dividing Fractions

1. division problem $\frac{1}{5} \times \frac{7}{4} =$ answer

2. division problem $\frac{1}{2} \times \frac{16}{13} =$ answer

3. division problem $\frac{2}{9} \times \frac{3}{1} =$ answer

4. division problem $\frac{1}{8} \times \frac{10}{9} =$ answer

5. division problem $\frac{7}{8} \times \frac{4}{1} =$ answer

6. division problem $\frac{5}{6} \times \frac{8}{3} =$ answer

Dividing Fractions

7 division problem $\frac{19}{20} \times \frac{2}{1} =$ answer

8 division problem $\frac{9}{5} \times \frac{3}{10} =$ answer

9 division problem $\frac{7}{3} \times \frac{8}{63} =$ answer

10 division problem $\frac{13}{4} \times \frac{2}{9} =$ answer

11 division problem $\frac{26}{5} \times \frac{4}{33} =$ answer

12 division problem $\frac{20}{3} \times \frac{8}{45} =$ answer

$\frac{1}{5} \div \frac{4}{7} =$	$\frac{1}{2} \div \frac{13}{16} =$	$\frac{7}{20}$	$\frac{16}{26}$
$\frac{2}{9} \div \frac{1}{3} =$	$\frac{1}{8} \div \frac{9}{10} =$	$\frac{6}{9}$	$\frac{10}{72}$
$\frac{7}{8} \div \frac{1}{4} =$	$\frac{5}{6} \div \frac{3}{8} =$	$\frac{28}{8}$	$\frac{27}{50}$
$\frac{19}{20} \div \frac{1}{2} =$	$1\frac{4}{5} \div 3\frac{1}{3} =$	$\frac{38}{20}$	$\frac{40}{18}$
$2\frac{1}{3} \div 7\frac{7}{8} =$	$3\frac{1}{4} \div 4\frac{1}{2} =$	$\frac{56}{189}$	$\frac{26}{36}$
$5\frac{1}{5} \div 8\frac{1}{4} =$	$6\frac{2}{3} \div 5\frac{5}{8} =$	$\frac{104}{165}$	$\frac{160}{135}$

Dividing Fractions
EMC 3076
© Evan-Moor Corp.

Dividing Fractions
EMC 3076
© Evan-Moor Corp.

Dividing Fractions
EMC 3076
© Evan-Moor Corp.

Dividing Fractions
EMC 3076
© Evan-Moor Corp.

Dividing Fractions
EMC 3076
© Evan-Moor Corp.

Dividing Fractions
EMC 3076
© Evan-Moor Corp.

Dividing Fractions
EMC 3076
© Evan-Moor Corp.

Dividing Fractions
EMC 3076
© Evan-Moor Corp.

Dividing Fractions
EMC 3076
© Evan-Moor Corp.

Dividing Fractions
EMC 3076
© Evan-Moor Corp.

Dividing Fractions
EMC 3076
© Evan-Moor Corp.

Dividing Fractions
EMC 3076
© Evan-Moor Corp.

Dividing Fractions
EMC 3076
© Evan-Moor Corp.

Dividing Fractions
EMC 3076
© Evan-Moor Corp.

Dividing Fractions
EMC 3076
© Evan-Moor Corp.

Dividing Fractions
EMC 3076
© Evan-Moor Corp.

Dividing Fractions
EMC 3076
© Evan-Moor Corp.

Dividing Fractions
EMC 3076
© Evan-Moor Corp.

Dividing Fractions
EMC 3076
© Evan-Moor Corp.

Dividing Fractions
EMC 3076
© Evan-Moor Corp.

Dividing Fractions
EMC 3076
© Evan-Moor Corp.

Dividing Fractions
EMC 3076
© Evan-Moor Corp.

Dividing Fractions
EMC 3076
© Evan-Moor Corp.

Dividing Fractions
EMC 3076
© Evan-Moor Corp.

Take It to Your Seat Centers

Order of Operations

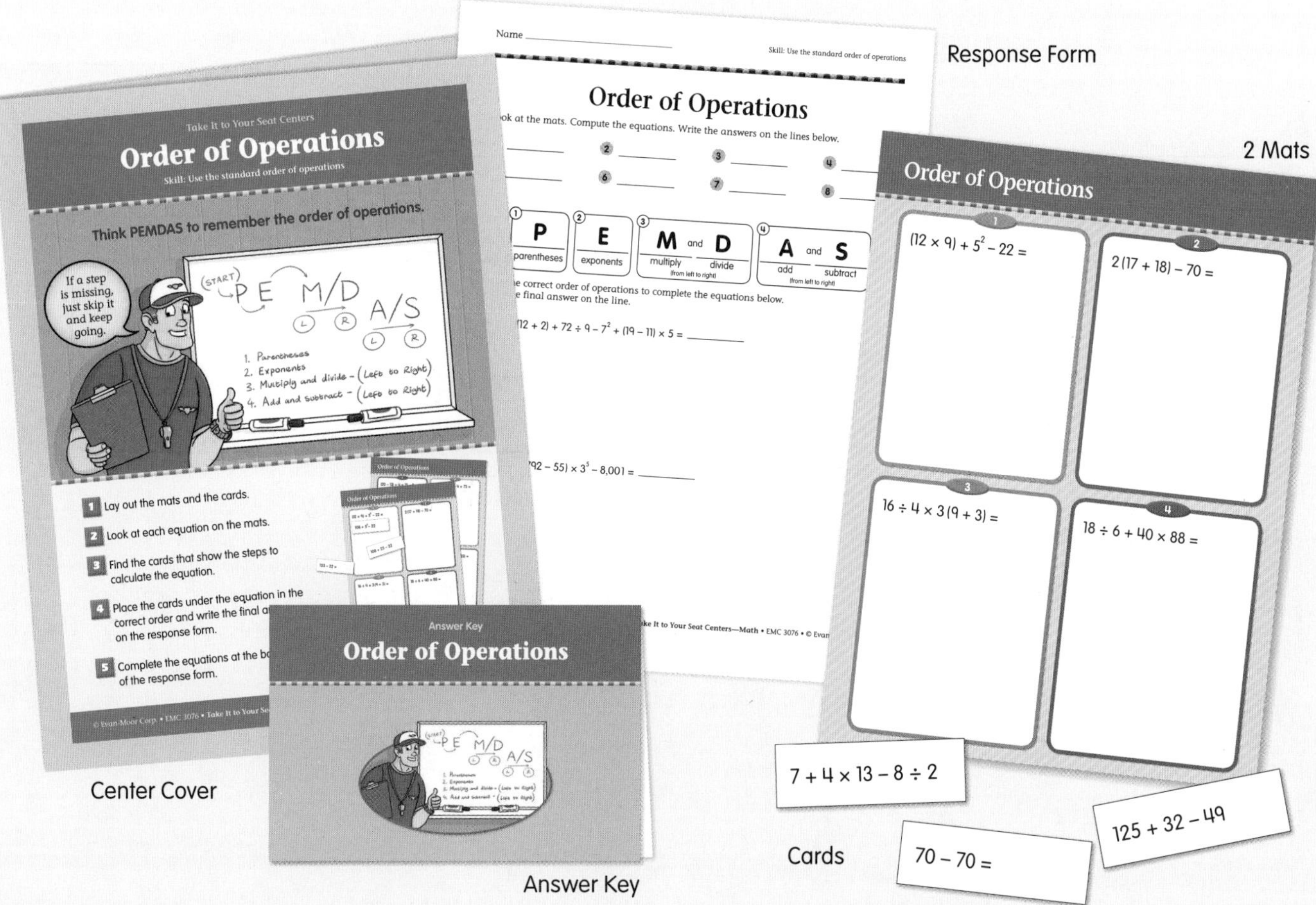

Skill: Use the standard order of operations to solve multistep equations

Steps to Follow

1. **Prepare the center.** (See page 3.)
2. **Introduce the center.** State the goal. Say: *You will find the cards that show the steps to solve each equation and place them below the equation in the correct order.*
3. **Teach the skill.** Demonstrate how to use the center with individual students or small groups.
4. **Practice the skill.** Have students use the center independently or with a partner.

Contents

Name ______________________ Skill: Use the standard order of operations

Order of Operations

Look at the mats. Compute the equations. Write the answers on the lines below.

1 __________ 2 __________ 3 __________ 4 __________

5 __________ 6 __________ 7 __________ 8 __________

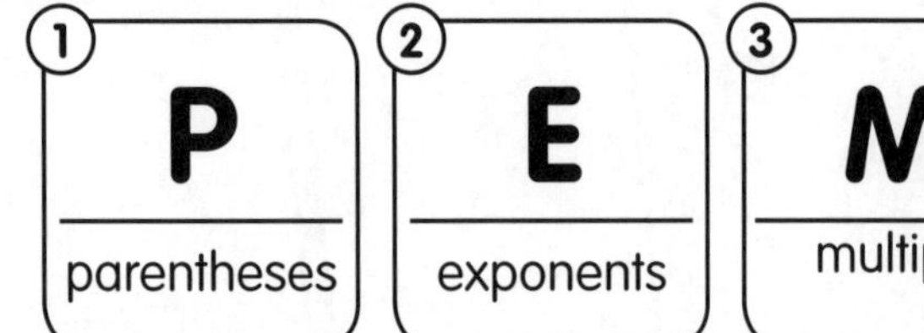

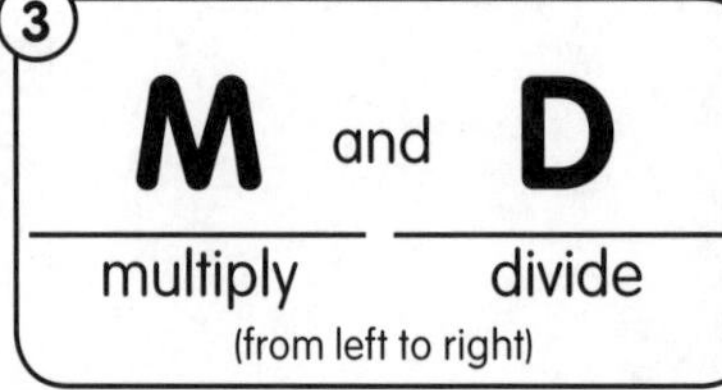

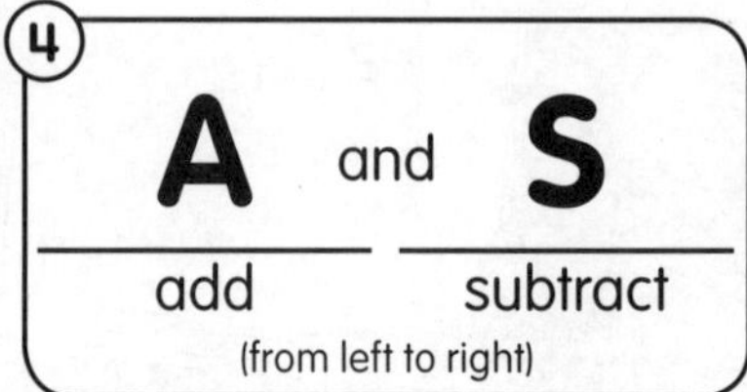

Show the correct order of operations to complete the equations below.
Write the final answer on the line.

1 $4(12 + 2) + 72 \div 9 - 7^2 + (19 - 11) \times 5 =$ __________

2 $13 \times (792 - 55) \times 3^5 - 8{,}001 =$ __________

Take It to Your Seat Centers

Order of Operations

Skill: Use the standard order of operations

1. Lay out the mats and the cards.
2. Look at each equation on the mats.
3. Find the cards that show the steps to calculate the equation.
4. Place the cards under the equation in the correct order and write the final answer on the response form.
5. Complete the equations at the bottom of the response form.

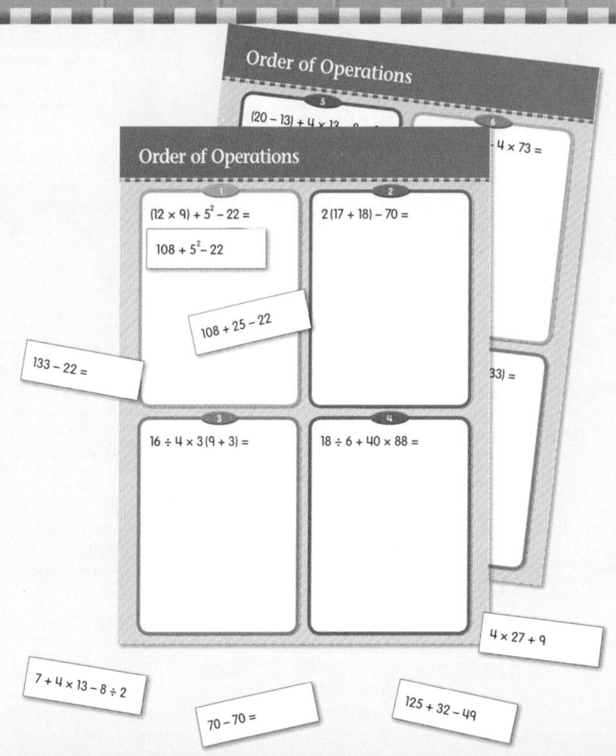

Answer Key

Order of Operations

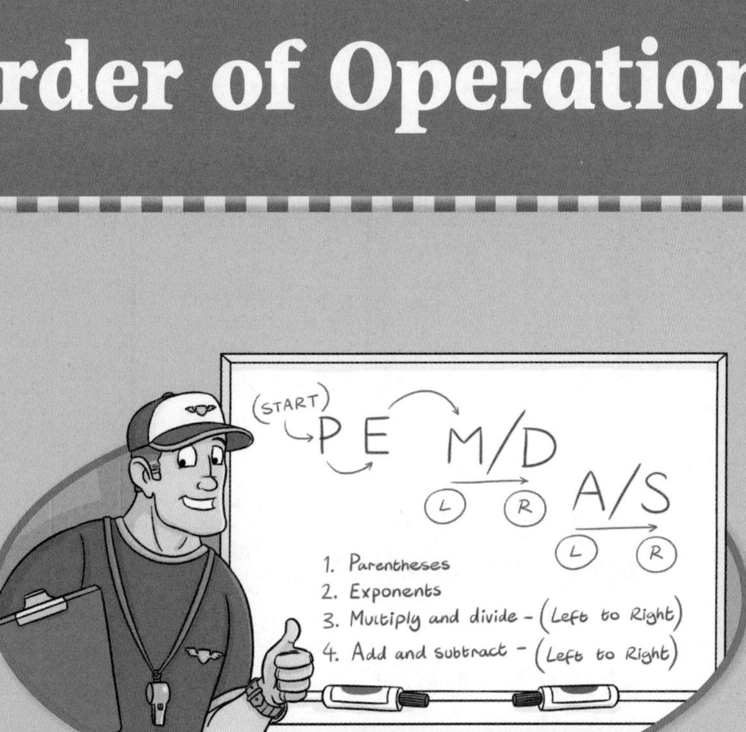

(fold)

Response Form

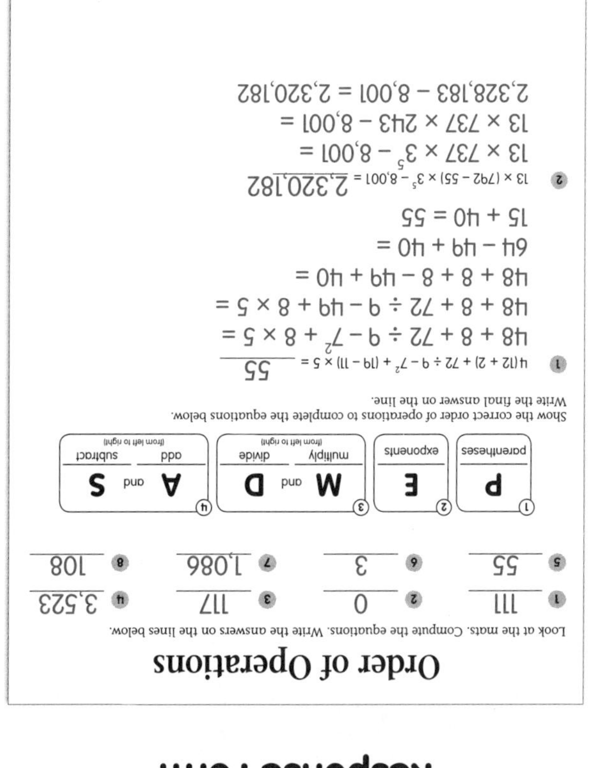

Order of Operations

Look at the mats. Compute the equations. Write the answers on the lines below.

1 111   2 0   3 117   4 3,523

5 55   6 3   7 1,086   8 108

1 **P** parentheses   2 **E** exponents   3 **M** and **D** multiply divide (from left to right)   4 **A** and **S** add subtract (from left to right)

Show the correct order of operations to complete the equations below. Write the final answer on the line.

1 $4(12 + 2) + 72 \div 9 - 7^2 + (19 - 11) \times 5 =$ 55

$48 + 8 + 72 \div 9 - 7^2 + 8 \times 5 =$

$48 + 8 + 72 \div 9 - 49 + 8 \times 5 =$

$48 + 8 + 8 - 49 + 40 =$

$64 - 49 + 40 =$

$15 + 40 = 55$

2 $13 \times (792 - 55) \times 3^5 - 8{,}001 =$ 2,320,182

$13 \times 737 \times 3^5 - 8{,}001 =$

$13 \times 737 \times 243 - 8{,}001 =$

$2{,}328{,}183 - 8{,}001 = 2{,}320{,}182$

Answer Key

Order of Operations

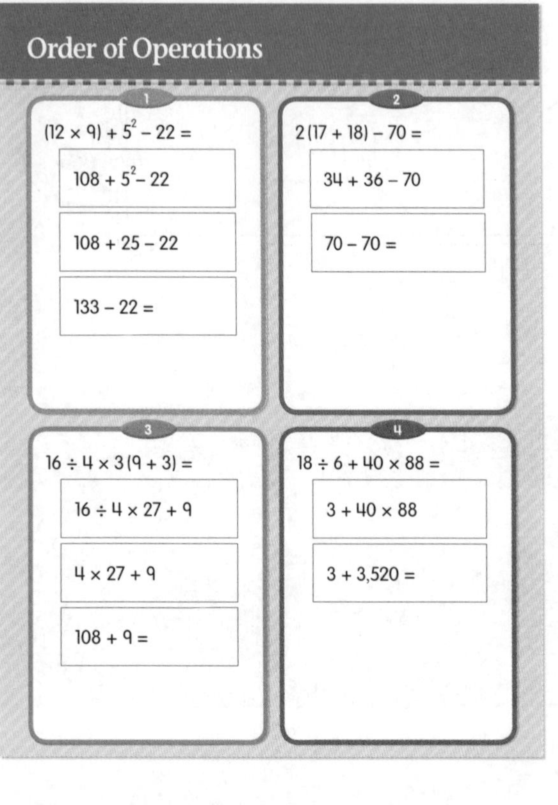

Order of Operations

1

$(12 \times 9) + 5^2 - 22 =$

$108 + 5^2 - 22$

$108 + 25 - 22$

$133 - 22 =$

2

$2(17 + 18) - 70 =$

$34 + 36 - 70$

$70 - 70 =$

3

$16 \div 4 \times 3(9 + 3) =$

$16 \div 4 \times 27 + 9$

$4 \times 27 + 9$

$108 + 9 =$

4

$18 \div 6 + 40 \times 88 =$

$3 + 40 \times 88$

$3 + 3{,}520 =$

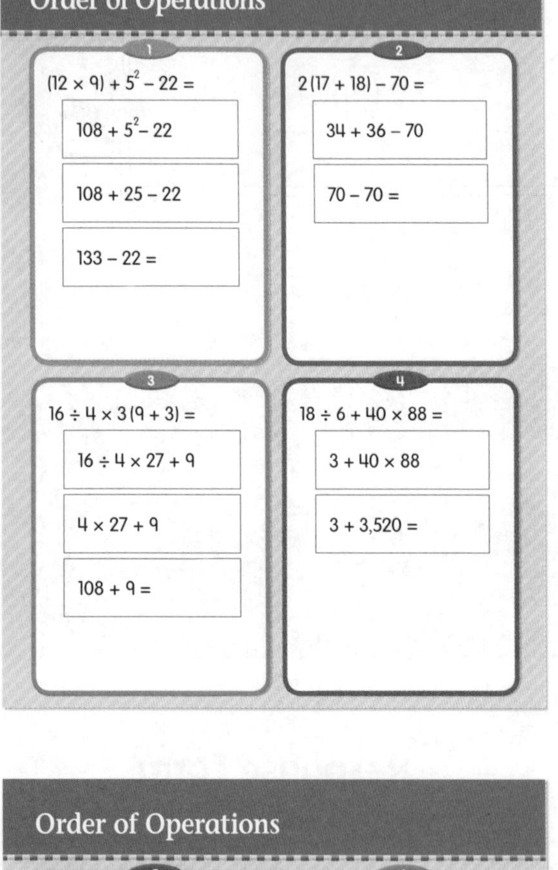

Order of Operations

5

$(20 - 13) + 4 \times 13 - 8 \div 2 =$

$7 + 4 \times 13 - 8 \div 2$

$7 + 52 - 8 \div 2$

$7 + 52 - 4$

$59 - 4 =$

6

$852 \div 3 + 11 - 4 \times 73 =$

$284 + 11 - 4 \times 73$

$284 + 11 - 292$

$295 - 292 =$

7

$6^4 - 216 + 18 \div 3 =$

$1{,}296 - 216 + 18 \div 3$

$1{,}296 - 216 + 6$

$1{,}080 + 6 =$

8

$5^3 + 4 \times 8 - (16 + 33) =$

$5^3 + 4 \times 8 - 49$

$125 + 4 \times 8 - 49$

$125 + 32 - 49$

$157 - 49 =$

Order of Operations

1

$(12 \times 9) + 5^2 - 22 =$

2

$2(17 + 18) - 70 =$

3

$16 \div 4 \times 3(9 + 3) =$

4

$18 \div 6 + 40 \times 88 =$

Order of Operations

5

$(20 - 13) + 4 \times 13 - 8 \div 2 =$

6

$852 \div 3 + 11 - 4 \times 73 =$

7

$6^4 - 216 + 18 \div 3 =$

8

$5^3 + 4 \times 8 - (16 + 33) =$

$108 + 5^2 - 22$	$3 + 40 \times 88$	$295 - 292 =$
$108 + 25 - 22$	$3 + 3{,}520 =$	$1{,}296 - 216 + 18 \div 3$
$133 - 22 =$	$7 + 4 \times 13 - 8 \div 2$	$1{,}296 - 216 + 6$
$34 + 36 - 70$	$7 + 52 - 8 \div 2$	$1{,}080 + 6 =$
$70 - 70 =$	$7 + 52 - 4$	$5^3 + 4 \times 8 - 49$
$16 \div 4 \times 27 + 9$	$59 - 4 =$	$125 + 4 \times 8 - 49$
$4 \times 27 + 9$	$284 + 11 - 4 \times 73$	$125 + 32 - 49$
$108 + 9 =$	$284 + 11 - 292$	$157 - 49 =$

Order of Operations
EMC 3076
© Evan-Moor Corp.

Order of Operations
EMC 3076
© Evan-Moor Corp.

Order of Operations
EMC 3076
© Evan-Moor Corp.

Order of Operations
EMC 3076
© Evan-Moor Corp.

Order of Operations
EMC 3076
© Evan-Moor Corp.

Order of Operations
EMC 3076
© Evan-Moor Corp.

Order of Operations
EMC 3076
© Evan-Moor Corp.

Order of Operations
EMC 3076
© Evan-Moor Corp.

Order of Operations
EMC 3076
© Evan-Moor Corp.

Order of Operations
EMC 3076
© Evan-Moor Corp.

Order of Operations
EMC 3076
© Evan-Moor Corp.

Order of Operations
EMC 3076
© Evan-Moor Corp.

Order of Operations
EMC 3076
© Evan-Moor Corp.

Order of Operations
EMC 3076
© Evan-Moor Corp.

Order of Operations
EMC 3076
© Evan-Moor Corp.

Order of Operations
EMC 3076
© Evan-Moor Corp.

Order of Operations
EMC 3076
© Evan-Moor Corp.

Order of Operations
EMC 3076
© Evan-Moor Corp.

Order of Operations
EMC 3076
© Evan-Moor Corp.

Order of Operations
EMC 3076
© Evan-Moor Corp.

Order of Operations
EMC 3076
© Evan-Moor Corp.

Order of Operations
EMC 3076
© Evan-Moor Corp.

Order of Operations
EMC 3076
© Evan-Moor Corp.

Order of Operations
EMC 3076
© Evan-Moor Corp.

Algebra

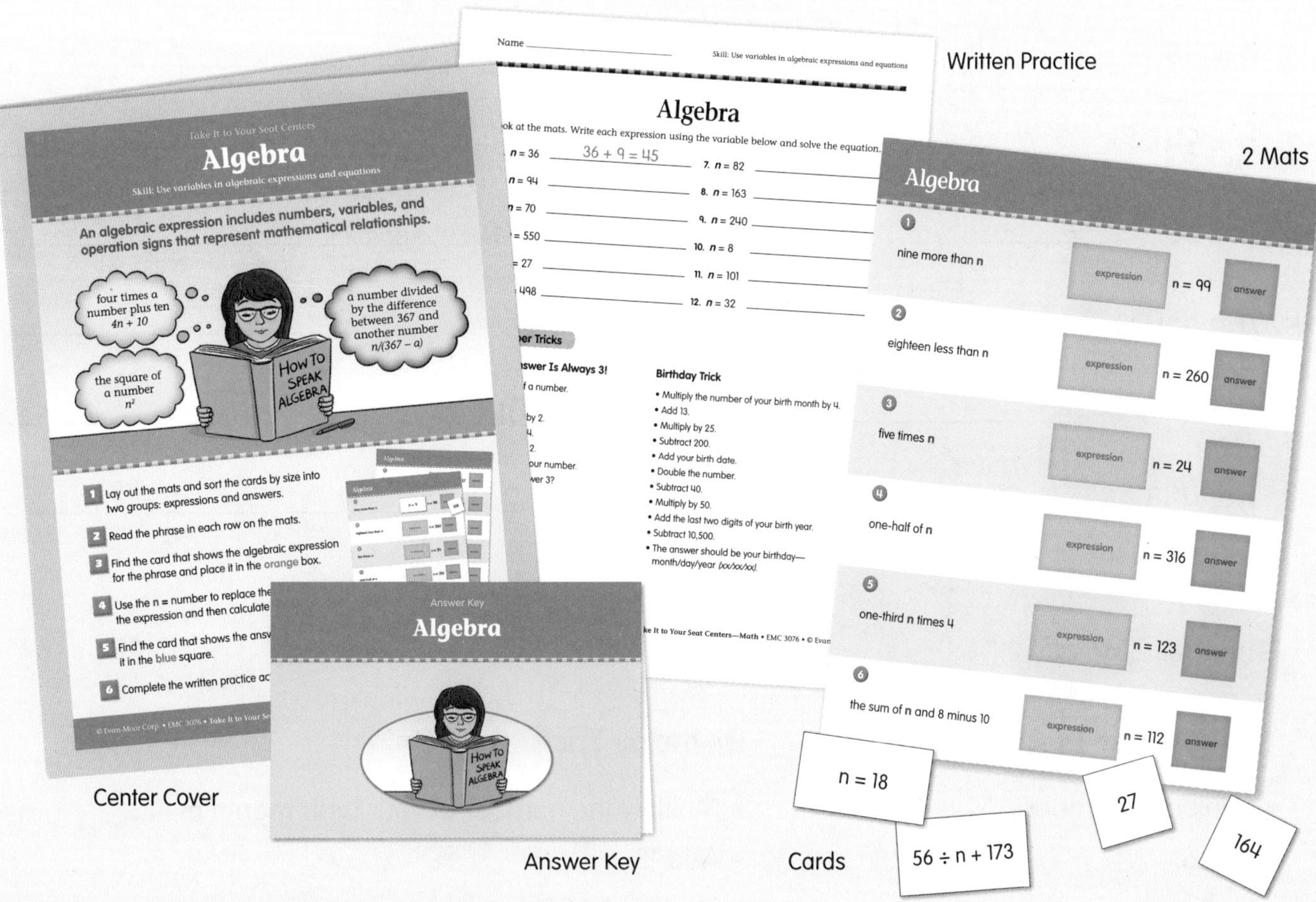

Skill: Use variables in algebraic expressions and equations

Steps to Follow

1. **Prepare the center.** (See page 3.)
2. **Introduce the center.** State the goal. Say: *You will convert each mathematical phrase to an algebraic expression and then replace the variable to solve the equation.*
3. **Teach the skill.** Demonstrate how to use the center with individual students or small groups.
4. **Practice the skill.** Have students use the center independently or with a partner.

Contents

Algebra

Look at the mats. Write each expression using the variable below and solve the equation.

1. $n = 36$ 36 + 9 = 45
2. $n = 94$ ____________________
3. $n = 70$ ____________________
4. $n = 550$ ____________________
5. $n = 27$ ____________________
6. $n = 498$ ____________________
7. $n = 82$ ____________________
8. $n = 163$ ____________________
9. $n = 240$ ____________________
10. $n = 8$ ____________________
11. $n = 101$ ____________________
12. $n = 32$ ____________________

Number Tricks

The Answer Is Always 3!

- Think of a number.
- Add 5.
- Multiply by 2.
- Subtract 4.
- Divide by 2.
- Subtract your number.
- Is the answer 3?

Birthday Trick

- Multiply the number of your birth month by 4.
- Add 13.
- Multiply by 25.
- Subtract 200.
- Add your birth date.
- Double the number.
- Subtract 40.
- Multiply by 50.
- Add the last two digits of your birth year.
- Subtract 10,500.
- The answer should be your birthday—month/day/year *(xx/xx/xx)*.

Algebra

Skill: Use variables in algebraic expressions and equations

An algebraic expression includes numbers, variables, and operation signs that represent mathematical relationships.

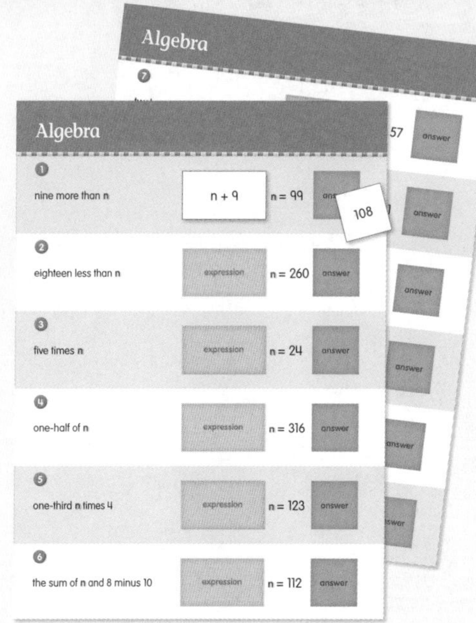

1. Lay out the mats and sort the cards by size into two groups: expressions and answers.
2. Read the phrase in each row on the mats.
3. Find the card that shows the algebraic expression for the phrase and place it in the **orange** box.
4. Use the **n =** number to replace the variable in the expression and then calculate the answer.
5. Find the card that shows the answer and place it in the **blue** square.
6. Complete the written practice activity.

Algebra

Answer Key

(fold)

Written Practice

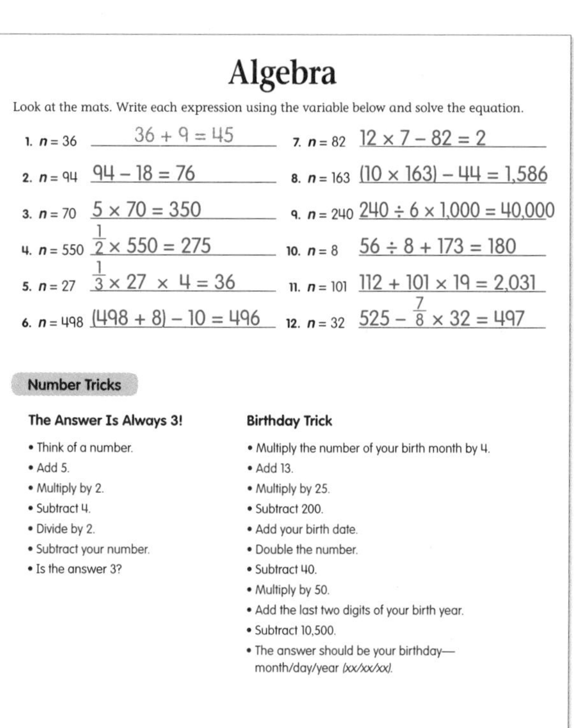

Algebra

Look at the mats. Write each expression using the variable below and solve the equation.

1. $n = 36$ $36 + 9 = 45$
2. $n = 94$ $94 - 18 = 76$
3. $n = 70$ $5 \times 70 = 350$
4. $n = 550$ $\frac{1}{2} \times 550 = 275$
5. $n = 27$ $\frac{1}{3} \times 27 \times 4 = 36$
6. $n = 498$ $(498 + 8) - 10 = 496$
7. $n = 82$ $12 \times 7 - 82 = 2$
8. $n = 163$ $(10 \times 163) - 44 = 1{,}586$
9. $n = 240$ $240 \div 6 \times 1{,}000 = 40{,}000$
10. $n = 8$ $56 \div 8 + 173 = 180$
11. $n = 101$ $112 + 101 \times 19 = 2{,}031$
12. $n = 32$ $525 - \frac{7}{8} \times 32 = 497$

Number Tricks

The Answer Is Always 3!

- Think of a number.
- Add 5.
- Multiply by 2.
- Subtract 4.
- Divide by 2.
- Subtract your number.
- Is the answer 3?

Birthday Trick

- Multiply the number of your birth month by 4.
- Add 13.
- Multiply by 25.
- Subtract 200.
- Add your birth date.
- Double the number.
- Subtract 40.
- Multiply by 50.
- Add the last two digits of your birth year.
- Subtract 10,500.
- The answer should be your birthday—month/day/year *(xx/xx/xx)*.

Answer Key

Algebra

Algebra

#	Phrase	Expression	Value	Answer
1	nine more than **n**	$n + 9$	$n = 99$	108
2	eighteen less than **n**	$n - 18$	$n = 260$	242
3	five times **n**	$5n$	$n = 24$	120
4	one-half of **n**	$\frac{1}{2}n$	$n = 316$	158
5	one-third **n** times 4	$\frac{1}{3}n \times 4$	$n = 123$	164
6	the sum of **n** and 8 minus 10	$(n + 8) - 10$	$n = 112$	110

Algebra

#	Phrase	Expression	Value	Answer
7	twelve times 7 minus **n**	$12 \times 7 - n$	$n = 57$	27
8	forty-four less than the product of 10 and **n**	$(10 \times n) - 44$	$n = 31$	266
9	**n** divided by 6 times 1,000	$n \div 6 \times 1{,}000$	$n = 60$	10,000
10	fifty-six divided by **n** plus 173	$56 \div n + 173$	$n = 2$	201
11	112 more than **n** times nineteen	$112 + n \times 19$	$n = 18$	454
12	$\frac{7}{8}$**n** less than 525	$525 - \frac{7}{8}n$	$n = 96$	441

Algebra

1 nine more than **n** — expression — $n = 99$ — answer

2 eighteen less than **n** — expression — $n = 260$ — answer

3 five times **n** — expression — $n = 24$ — answer

4 one-half of **n** — expression — $n = 316$ — answer

5 one-third **n** times 4 — expression — $n = 123$ — answer

6 the sum of **n** and 8 minus 10 — expression — $n = 112$ — answer

Algebra

7

twelve times 7 minus **n**

expression

n = 57

answer

8

forty-four less than the product of 10 and **n**

expression

n = 31

answer

9

n divided by 6 times 1,000

expression

n = 60

answer

10

fifty-six divided by **n** plus 173

expression

n = 2

answer

11

112 more than **n** times nineteen

expression

n = 18

answer

12

$\frac{7}{8}$**n** less than 525

expression

n = 96

answer

$n + 9$	$n - 18$	$5n$
$\frac{1}{2}n$	$\frac{1}{3}n \times 4$	$(n + 8) - 10$
$12 \times 7 - n$	$(10 \times n) - 44$	$n \div 6 \times 1{,}000$
$56 \div n + 173$	$112 + n \times 19$	$525 - \frac{7}{8}n$

108	242	120	158
110	27	266	10,000
454	441	164	201

Algebra
EMC 3076
© Evan-Moor Corp.

Algebra
EMC 3076
© Evan-Moor Corp.

Algebra
EMC 3076
© Evan-Moor Corp.

Algebra
EMC 3076
© Evan-Moor Corp.

Algebra
EMC 3076
© Evan-Moor Corp.

Algebra
EMC 3076
© Evan-Moor Corp.

Algebra
EMC 3076
© Evan-Moor Corp.

Algebra
EMC 3076
© Evan-Moor Corp.

Algebra
EMC 3076
© Evan-Moor Corp.

Algebra
EMC 3076
© Evan-Moor Corp.

Algebra
EMC 3076
© Evan-Moor Corp.

Algebra
EMC 3076
© Evan-Moor Corp.

Algebra
EMC 3076
© Evan-Moor Corp.

Algebra
EMC 3076
© Evan-Moor Corp.

Algebra
EMC 3076
© Evan-Moor Corp.

Algebra
EMC 3076
© Evan-Moor Corp.

Algebra
EMC 3076
© Evan-Moor Corp.

Algebra
EMC 3076
© Evan-Moor Corp.

Algebra
EMC 3076
© Evan-Moor Corp.

Algebra
EMC 3076
© Evan-Moor Corp.

Algebra
EMC 3076
© Evan-Moor Corp.

Algebra
EMC 3076
© Evan-Moor Corp.

Algebra
EMC 3076
© Evan-Moor Corp.

Algebra
EMC 3076
© Evan-Moor Corp.

Take It to Your Seat Centers

Complex Figures

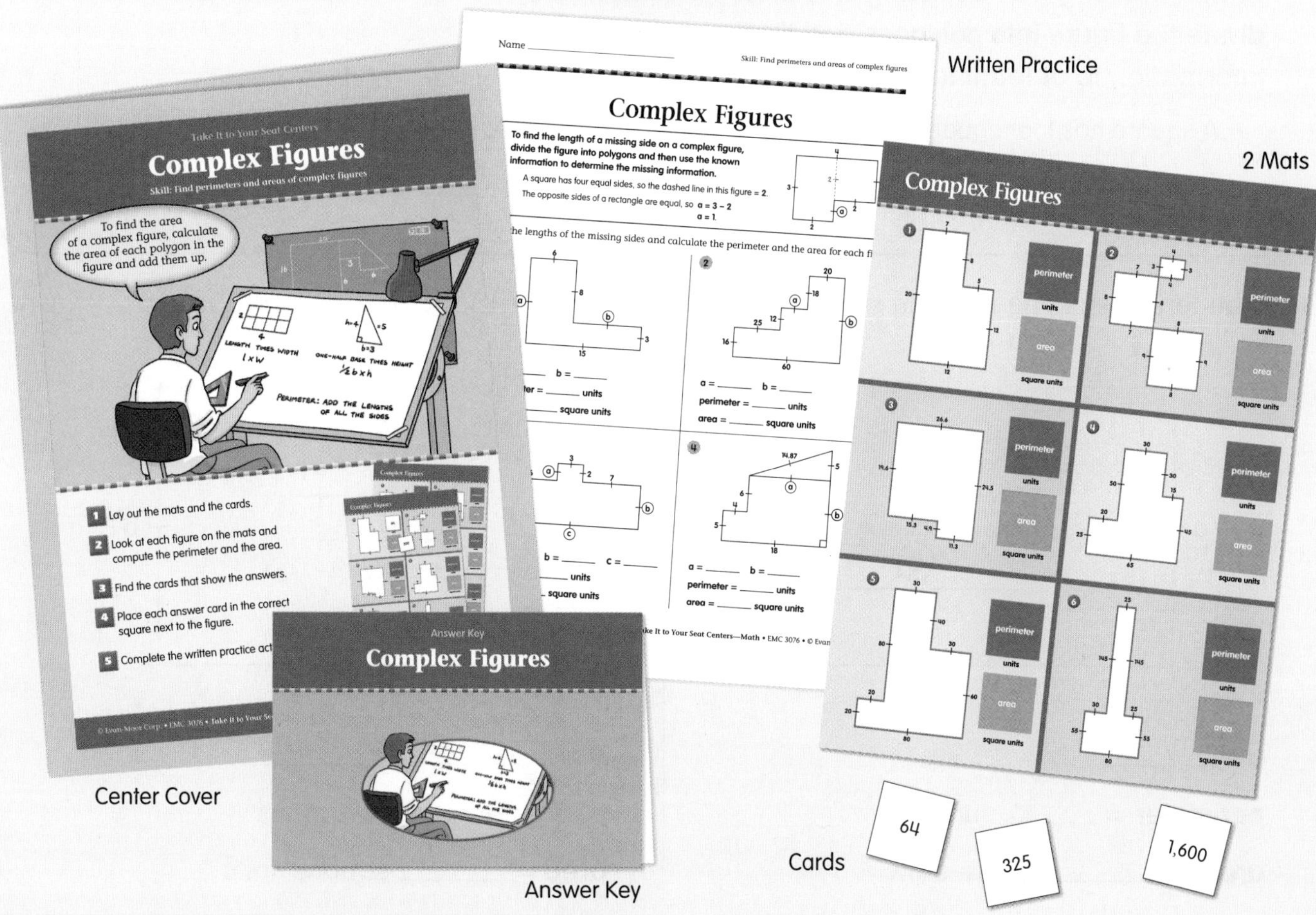

Skill: Find perimeters and areas of complex figures

Steps to Follow

1. **Prepare the center.** (See page 3.)
2. **Introduce the center.** State the goal. Say: *You will compute the perimeter and the area for each figure on the mats.*
3. **Teach the skill.** Demonstrate how to use the center with individual students or small groups.
4. **Practice the skill.** Have students use the center independently or with a partner.

Contents

Complex Figures

To find the length of a missing side on a complex figure, divide the figure into polygons and then use the known information to determine the missing information.

A square has four equal sides, so the dashed line in this figure = **2**.

The opposite sides of a rectangle are equal, so **a = 3 – 2**
a = 1.

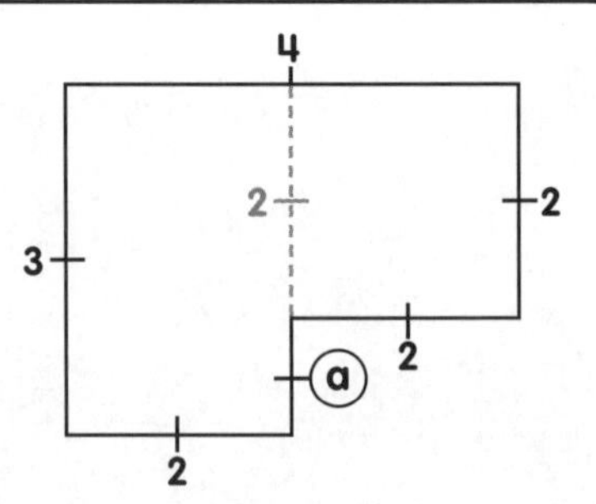

Find the lengths of the missing sides and calculate the perimeter and the area for each figure.

1

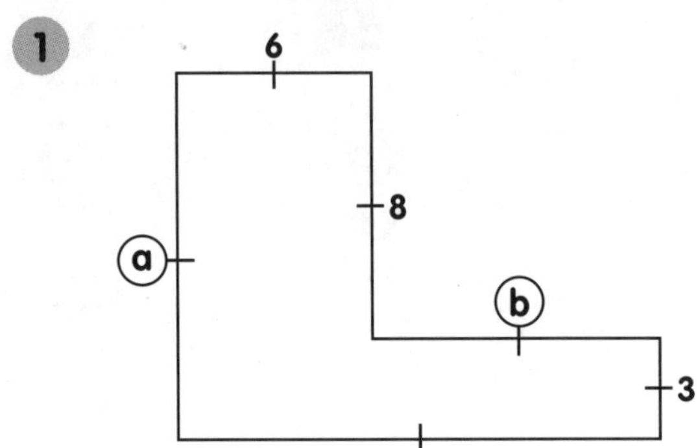

a = ______ **b =** ______

perimeter = ______ **units**

area = ______ **square units**

2

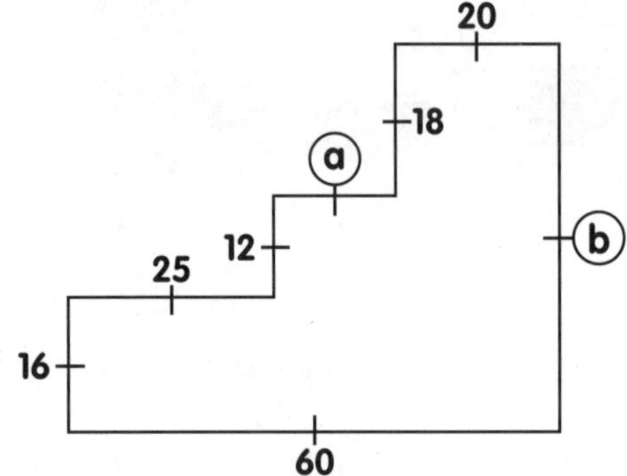

a = ______ **b =** ______

perimeter = ______ **units**

area = ______ **square units**

3

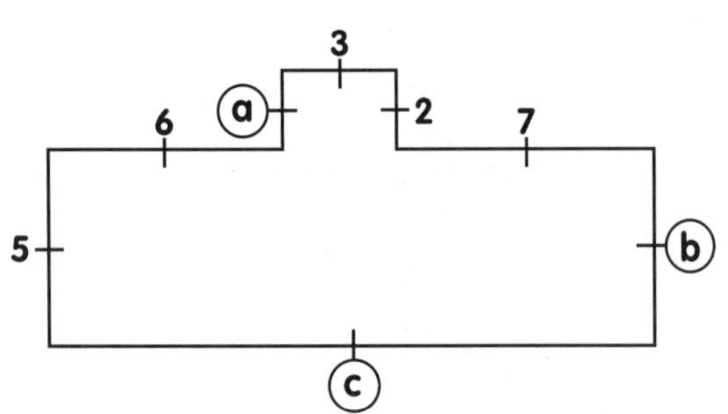

a = ______ **b =** ______ **c =** ______

perimeter = ______ **units**

area = ______ **square units**

4

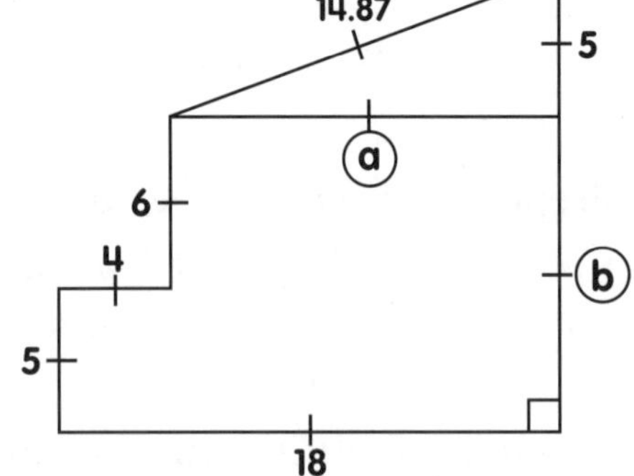

a = ______ **b =** ______

perimeter = ______ **units**

area = ______ **square units**

Complex Figures

Skill: Find perimeters and areas of complex figures

1. Lay out the mats and the cards.
2. Look at each figure on the mats and compute the perimeter and the area.
3. Find the cards that show the answers.
4. Place each answer card in the correct square next to the figure.
5. Complete the written practice activity.

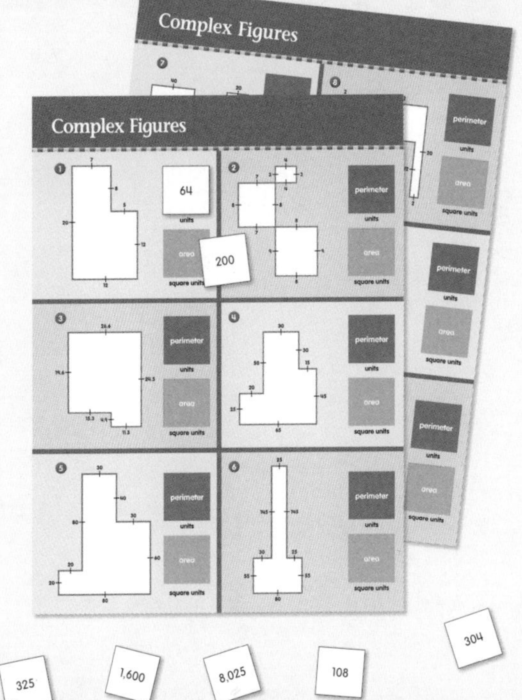

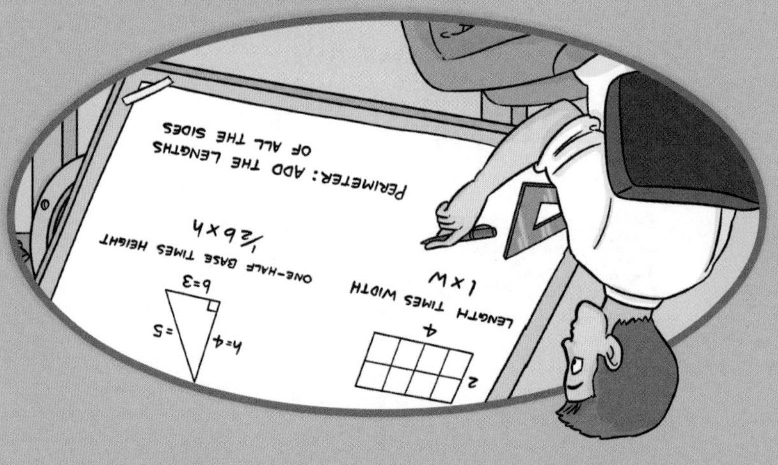

Complex Figures

Answer Key

(fold)

Written Practice

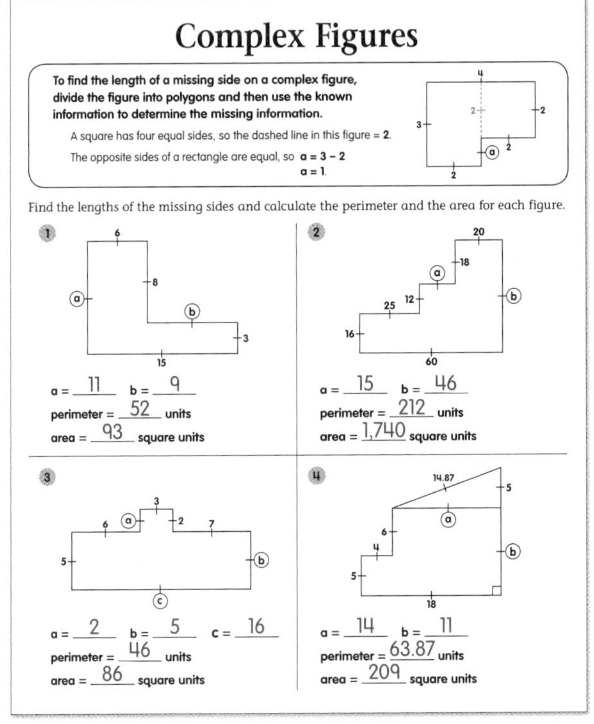

Complex Figures

To find the length of a missing side on a complex figure, divide the figure into polygons and then use the known information to determine the missing information.

A square has four equal sides, so the dashed line in this figure = **2**.

The opposite sides of a rectangle are equal, so **a = 3 – 2**
a = 1.

Find the lengths of the missing sides and calculate the perimeter and the area for each figure.

1

a = 11 b = 9
perimeter = 52 units
area = 93 square units

2

a = 15 b = 46
perimeter = 212 units
area = 1,740 square units

3

a = 2 b = 5 c = 16
perimeter = 46 units
area = 86 square units

4

a = 14 b = 11
perimeter = 63.87 units
area = 209 square units

Answer Key

Complex Figures

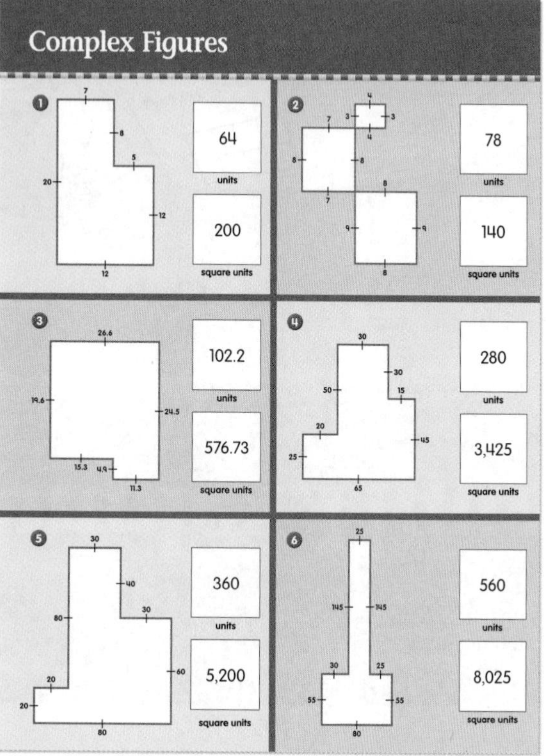

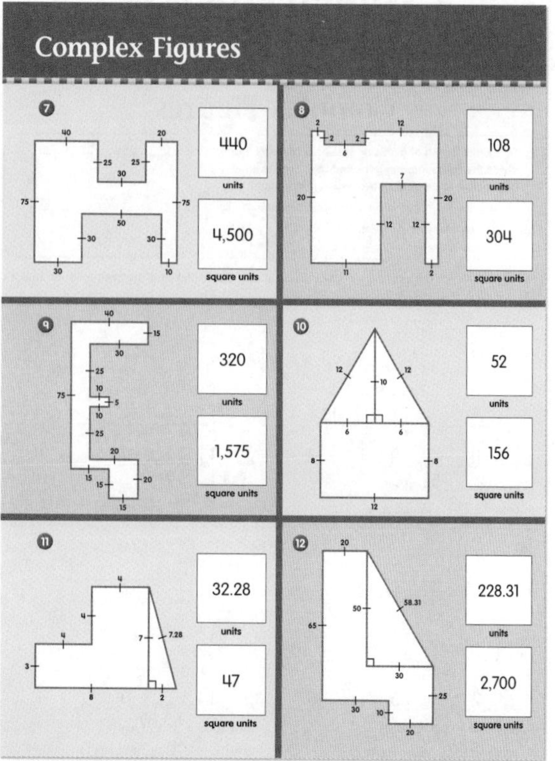

Complex Figures

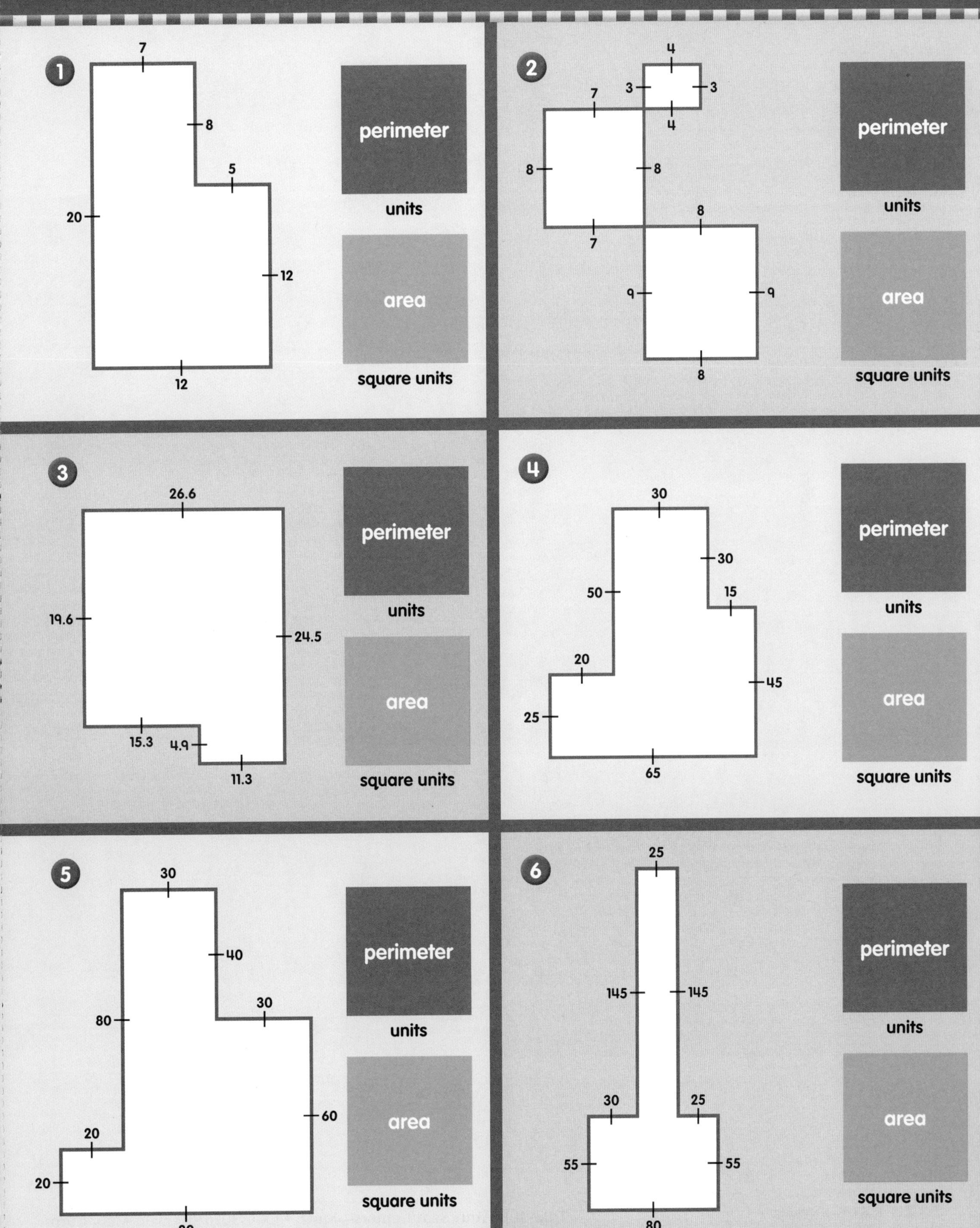

Complex Figures

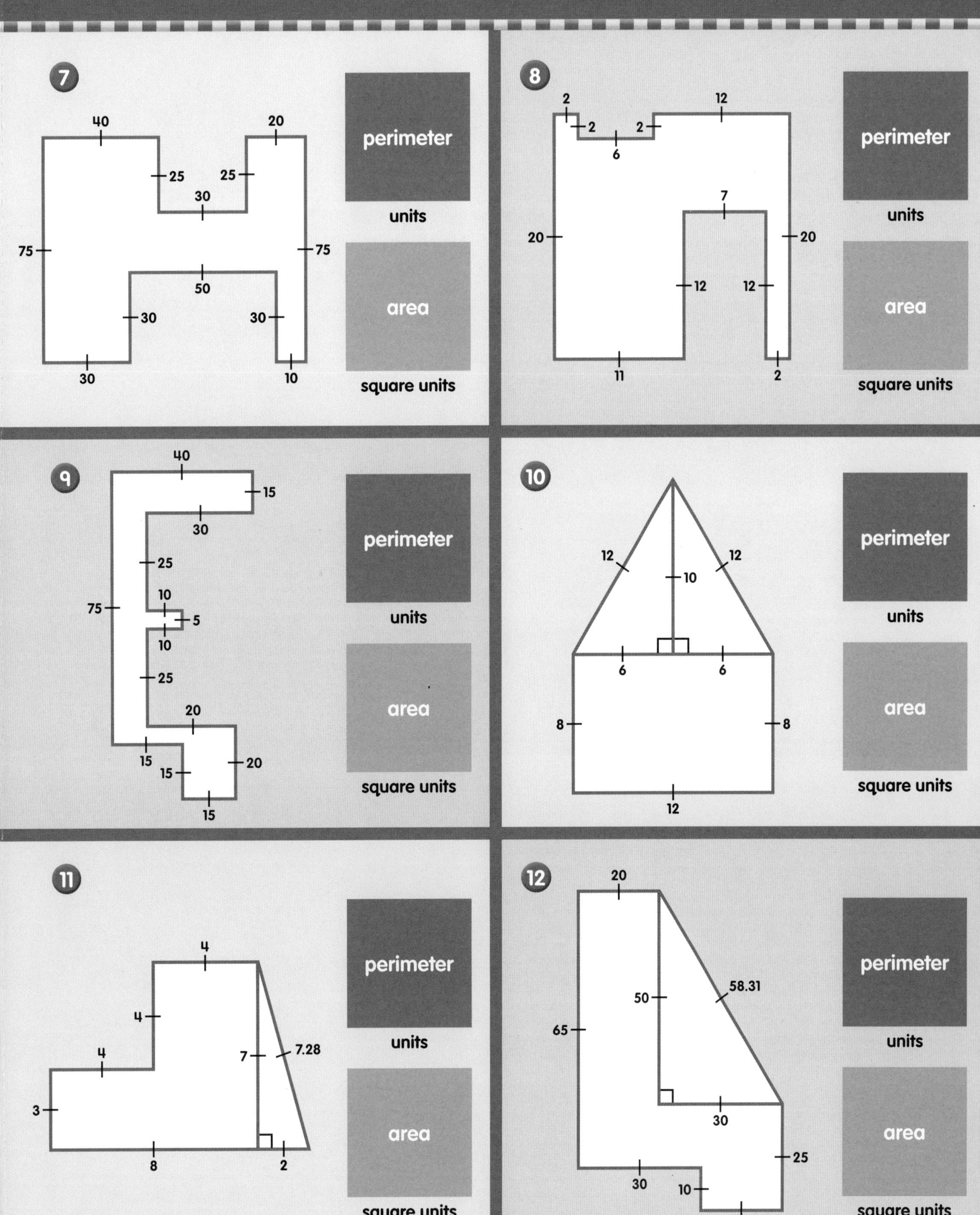

64	200	78	140
102.2	576.73	280	3,425
360	5,200	560	8,025
440	4,500	108	304
320	1,575	52	156
32.28	47	228.31	2,700

Complex Figures EMC 3076 © Evan-Moor Corp.	Complex Figures EMC 3076 © Evan-Moor Corp.	Complex Figures EMC 3076 © Evan-Moor Corp.	Complex Figures EMC 3076 © Evan-Moor Corp.
Complex Figures EMC 3076 © Evan-Moor Corp.	Complex Figures EMC 3076 © Evan-Moor Corp.	Complex Figures EMC 3076 © Evan-Moor Corp.	Complex Figures EMC 3076 © Evan-Moor Corp.
Complex Figures EMC 3076 © Evan-Moor Corp.	Complex Figures EMC 3076 © Evan-Moor Corp.	Complex Figures EMC 3076 © Evan-Moor Corp.	Complex Figures EMC 3076 © Evan-Moor Corp.
Complex Figures EMC 3076 © Evan-Moor Corp.	Complex Figures EMC 3076 © Evan-Moor Corp.	Complex Figures EMC 3076 © Evan-Moor Corp.	Complex Figures EMC 3076 © Evan-Moor Corp.
Complex Figures EMC 3076 © Evan-Moor Corp.	Complex Figures EMC 3076 © Evan-Moor Corp.	Complex Figures EMC 3076 © Evan-Moor Corp.	Complex Figures EMC 3076 © Evan-Moor Corp.
Complex Figures EMC 3076 © Evan-Moor Corp.	Complex Figures EMC 3076 © Evan-Moor Corp.	Complex Figures EMC 3076 © Evan-Moor Corp.	Complex Figures EMC 3076 © Evan-Moor Corp.

Take It to Your Seat Centers

Graphs and Statistics

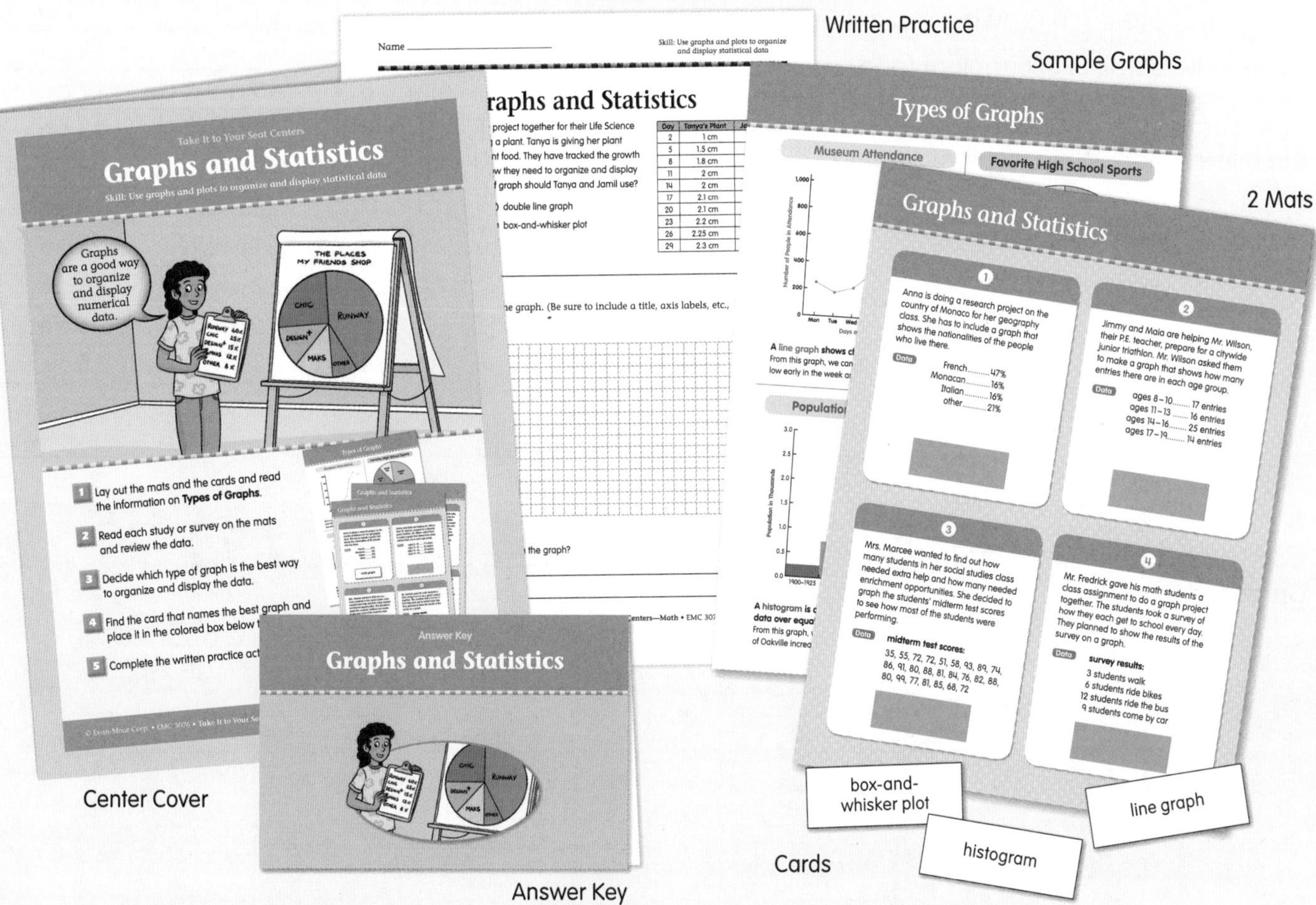

Skill: Use graphs and plots to organize and display statistical data

Steps to Follow

1. **Prepare the center.** (See page 3.)
2. **Introduce the center.** State the goal. Say: *You will read the data related to each study or survey on the mats and tell which kind of graph is the best way to organize and display the data.*
3. **Teach the skill.** Demonstrate how to use the center with individual students or small groups.
4. **Practice the skill.** Have students use the center independently or with a partner.

Contents

Name ______________________

Skill: Use graphs and plots to organize and display statistical data

Graphs and Statistics

Tanya and Jamil are doing a project together for their Life Science class. They are each growing a plant. Tanya is giving her plant water only. Jamil is using plant food. They have tracked the growth of each plant for a month. Now they need to organize and display the information. Which type of graph should Tanya and Jamil use?

Day	Tanya's Plant	Jamil's Plant
2	1 cm	1 cm
5	1.5 cm	1 cm
8	1.8 cm	1.2 cm
11	2 cm	1.3 cm
14	2 cm	1.5 cm
17	2.1 cm	1.9 cm
20	2.1 cm	2.1 cm
23	2.2 cm	2.3 cm
26	2.25 cm	2.5 cm
29	2.3 cm	2.5 cm

- ○ bar graph
- ○ double line graph
- ○ histogram
- ○ box-and-whisker plot

Explain why.

____

Use the grid below to build the graph. (Be sure to include a title, axis labels, etc., on your graph.)

What can Tanya and Jamil infer from the graph?

____

____

Take It to Your Seat Centers

Graphs and Statistics

Skill: Use graphs and plots to organize and display statistical data

Graphs are a good way to organize and display numerical data.

RUNWAY 40%
CHIC 25%
DESIGN+ 15%
MAKS 12%
OTHER 8%

THE PLACES MY FRIENDS SHOP

CHIC
RUNWAY
DESIGN+
MAKS
OTHER

1. Lay out the mats and the cards and read the information on **Types of Graphs**.
2. Read each study or survey on the mats and review the data.
3. Decide which type of graph is the best way to organize and display the data.
4. Find the card that names the best graph and place it in the colored box below the data.
5. Complete the written practice activity.

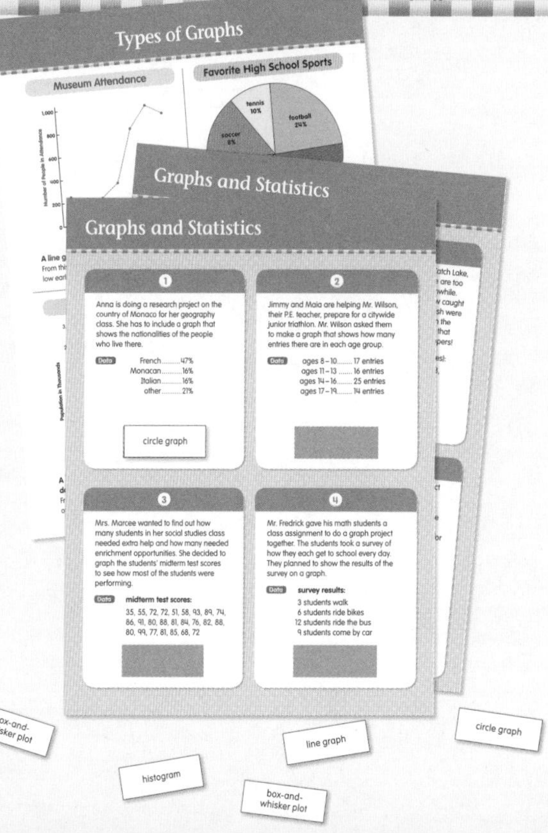

Graphs and Statistics

Answer Key

(fold)

Written Practice

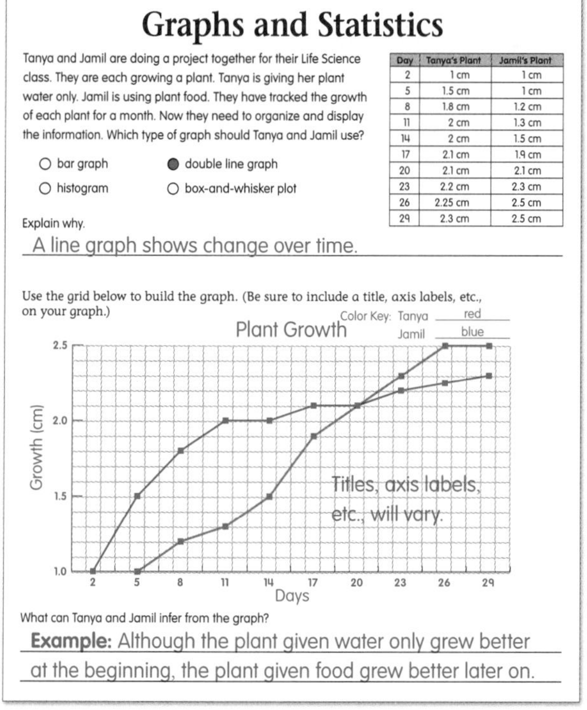

Graphs and Statistics

Tanya and Jamil are doing a project together for their Life Science class. They are each growing a plant. Tanya is giving her plant water only. Jamil is using plant food. They have tracked the growth of each plant for a month. Now they need to organize and display the information. Which type of graph should Tanya and Jamil use?

Day	Tanya's Plant	Jamil's Plant
2	1 cm	1 cm
5	1.5 cm	1 cm
8	1.8 cm	1.2 cm
11	2 cm	1.3 cm
14	2 cm	1.5 cm
17	2.1 cm	1.9 cm
20	2.1 cm	2.1 cm
23	2.2 cm	2.3 cm
26	2.25 cm	2.5 cm
29	2.3 cm	2.5 cm

○ bar graph
● double line graph
○ histogram
○ box-and-whisker plot

Explain why.

A line graph shows change over time.

Use the grid below to build the graph. (Be sure to include a title, axis labels, etc., on your graph.)

What can Tanya and Jamil infer from the graph?

Example: Although the plant given water only grew better at the beginning, the plant given food grew better later on.

Answer Key

Graphs and Statistics

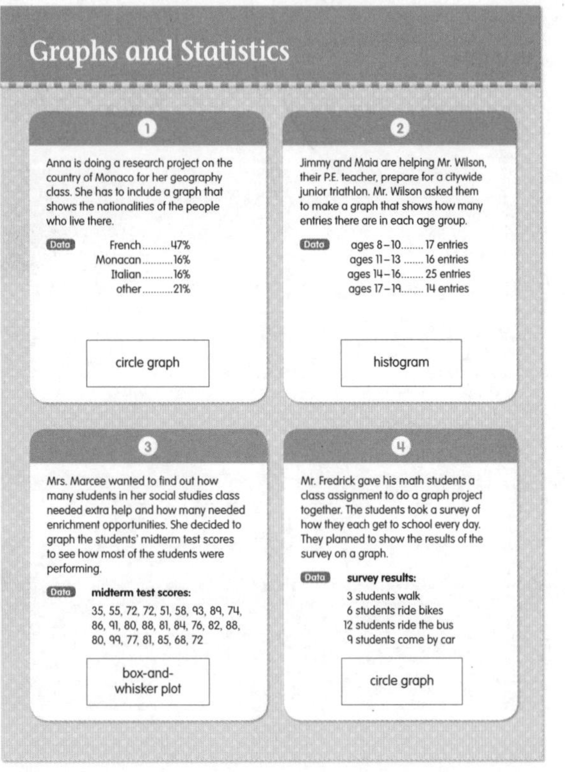

Graphs and Statistics

1

Anna is doing a research project on the country of Monaco for her geography class. She has to include a graph that shows the nationalities of the people who live there.

Data
French..........47%
Monacan..........16%
Italian..........16%
other..........21%

circle graph

2

Jimmy and Maia are helping Mr. Wilson, their P.E. teacher, prepare for a citywide junior triathlon. Mr. Wilson asked them to make a graph that shows how many entries there are in each age group.

Data
ages 8–10........ 17 entries
ages 11–13 .... 16 entries
ages 14–16........ 25 entries
ages 17–19........ 14 entries

histogram

3

Mrs. Marcee wanted to find out how many students in her social studies class needed extra help and how many needed enrichment opportunities. She decided to graph the students' midterm test scores to see how most of the students were performing.

Data **midterm test scores:**
35, 55, 72, 72, 51, 58, 93, 89, 74, 86, 91, 80, 88, 81, 84, 76, 82, 88, 80, 99, 77, 81, 85, 68, 72

box-and-whisker plot

4

Mr. Fredrick gave his math students a class assignment to do a graph project together. The students took a survey of how they each get to school every day. They planned to show the results of the survey on a graph.

Data **survey results:**
3 students walk
6 students ride bikes
12 students ride the bus
9 students come by car

circle graph

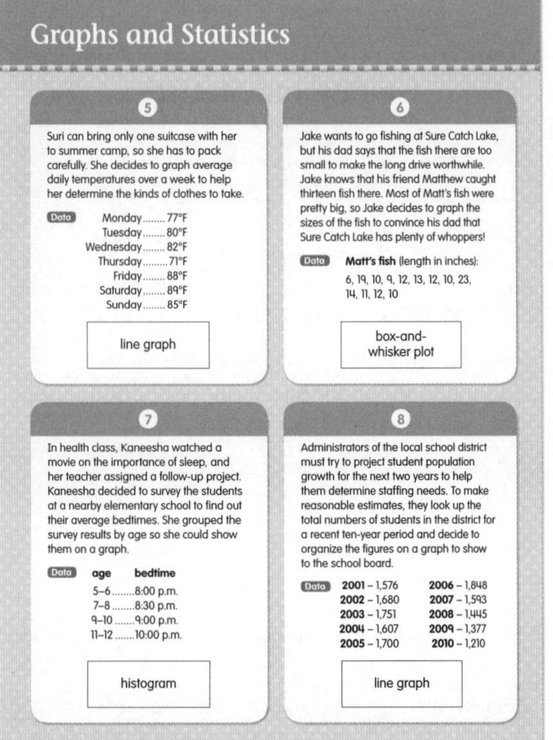

Graphs and Statistics

5

Suri can bring only one suitcase with her to summer camp, so she has to pack carefully. She decides to graph average daily temperatures over a week to help her determine the kinds of clothes to take.

Data
Monday........ 77°F
Tuesday........ 80°F
Wednesday........ 82°F
Thursday........ 71°F
Friday........ 88°F
Saturday........ 89°F
Sunday........ 85°F

line graph

6

Jake wants to go fishing at Sure Catch Lake, but his dad says that the fish there are too small to make the long drive worthwhile. Jake knows that his friend Matthew caught thirteen fish there. Most of Matt's fish were pretty big, so Jake decides to graph the sizes of the fish to convince his dad that Sure Catch Lake has plenty of whoppers!

Data **Matt's fish** (length in inches):
6, 19, 10, 9, 12, 13, 12, 10, 23, 14, 11, 12, 10

box-and-whisker plot

7

In health class, Kaneesha watched a movie on the importance of sleep, and her teacher assigned a follow-up project. Kaneesha decided to survey the students at a nearby elementary school to find out their average bedtimes. She grouped the survey results by age so she could show them on a graph.

Data

age	bedtime
5–6	8:00 p.m.
7–8	8:30 p.m.
9–10	9:00 p.m.
11–12	10:00 p.m.

histogram

8

Administrators of the local school district must try to project student population growth for the next two years to help them determine staffing needs. To make reasonable estimates, they look up the total numbers of students in the district for a recent ten-year period and decide to organize the figures on a graph to show to the school board.

Data
2001 – 1,576 **2006** – 1,848
2002 – 1,680 **2007** – 1,593
2003 – 1,751 **2008** – 1,445
2004 – 1,607 **2009** – 1,377
2005 – 1,700 **2010** – 1,210

line graph

Types of Graphs

Museum Attendance

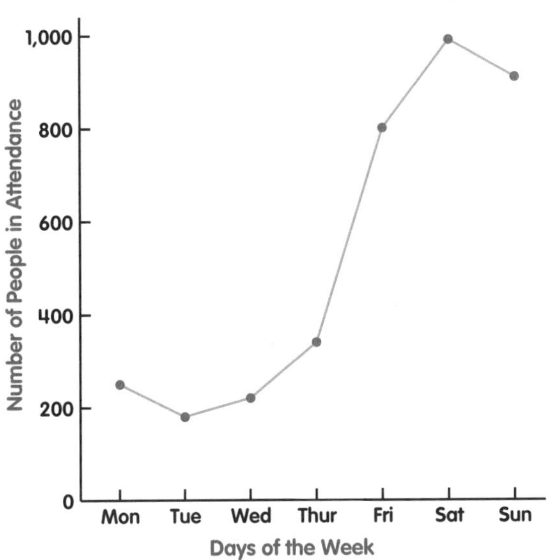

A line graph shows change over time.
From this graph, we can infer that attendance is low early in the week and high on the weekends.

Favorite High School Sports

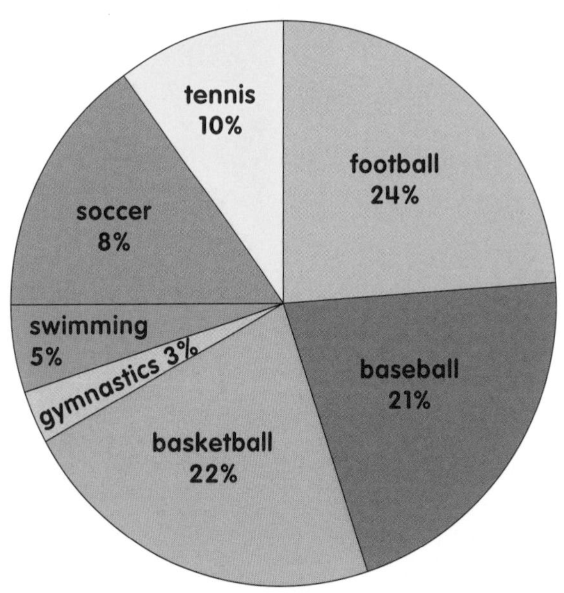

A circle graph compares parts of a whole.
From this graph, we can infer that football is the most favorite high school sport.

Population of Oakville

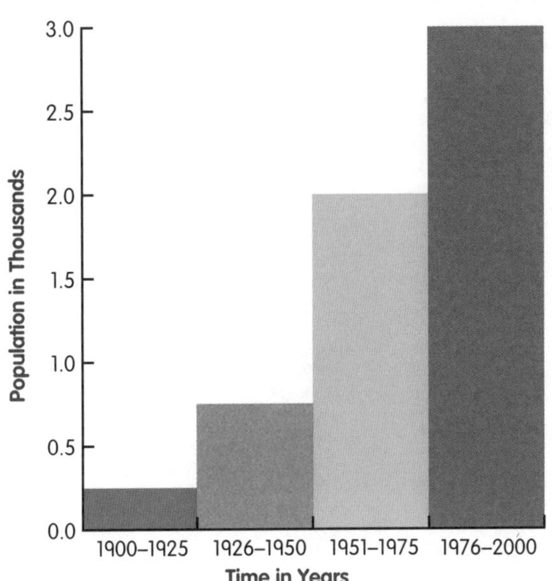

A histogram is a bar graph that shows like data over equal intervals or spans of time.
From this graph, we can infer that the population of Oakville increased the most from 1950 to 1975.

Lengths of Pet Snakes

Data: the lengths (in inches) of 11 pet snakes
11, 5, 13, 7, 9, 22, 13, 7, 8, 12, 13

Step 1 Arrange the data from lowest to highest:
5, 7, 7, 8, 9, 11, 12, 13, 13, 13, 22

Step 2 Find the median value (middle number): **11**

Step 3 Find the median range: lower median = **7**; upper median = **13**

Step 4 Plot the data on a number line: Draw a box between the lower and upper medians, with a line at the median. Draw lines (whiskers) out to the lowest and highest data values.

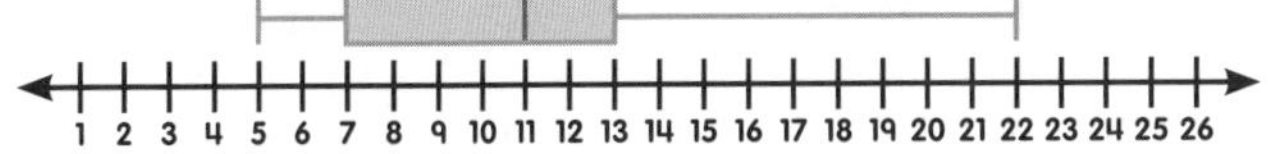

A box-and-whisker plot shows the median values and the outliers in a set of data.
From this plot, we can infer that most of the snakes are 7 to 13 inches long, with a median length of 11 inches.

Graphs and Statistics

1

Anna is doing a research project on the country of Monaco for her geography class. She has to include a graph that shows the nationalities of the people who live there.

Data

French 47%
Monacan 16%
Italian 16%
other 21%

2

Jimmy and Maia are helping Mr. Wilson, their P.E. teacher, prepare for a citywide junior triathlon. Mr. Wilson asked them to make a graph that shows how many entries there are in each age group.

Data

ages 8 – 10 .... 17 entries
ages 11 – 13 .... 16 entries
ages 14 – 16 .... 25 entries
ages 17 – 19 .... 14 entries

3

Mrs. Marcee wanted to find out how many students in her social studies class needed extra help and how many needed enrichment opportunities. She decided to graph the students' midterm test scores to see how most of the students were performing.

Data **midterm test scores:**

35, 55, 72, 72, 51, 58, 93, 89, 74, 86, 91, 80, 88, 81, 84, 76, 82, 88, 80, 99, 77, 81, 85, 68, 72

4

Mr. Fredrick gave his math students a class assignment to do a graph project together. The students took a survey of how they each get to school every day. They planned to show the results of the survey on a graph.

Data **survey results:**

3 students walk
6 students ride bikes
12 students ride the bus
9 students come by car

Graphs and Statistics

5

Suri can bring only one suitcase with her to summer camp, so she has to pack carefully. She decides to graph average daily temperatures over a week to help her determine the kinds of clothes to take.

Data

Monday........ 77°F
Tuesday........ 80°F
Wednesday........ 82°F
Thursday.........71°F
Friday........ 88°F
Saturday........ 89°F
Sunday........ 85°F

6

Jake wants to go fishing at Sure Catch Lake, but his dad says that the fish there are too small to make the long drive worthwhile. Jake knows that his friend Matthew caught thirteen fish there. Most of Matt's fish were pretty big, so Jake decides to graph the sizes of the fish to convince his dad that Sure Catch Lake has plenty of whoppers!

Data **Matt's fish** (length in inches):

6, 19, 10, 9, 12, 13, 12, 10, 23, 14, 11, 12, 10

7

In health class, Kaneesha watched a movie on the importance of sleep, and her teacher assigned a follow-up project. Kaneesha decided to survey the students at a nearby elementary school to find out their average bedtimes. She grouped the survey results by age so she could show them on a graph.

Data

age	bedtime
5–6	8:00 p.m.
7–8	8:30 p.m.
9–10	9:00 p.m.
11–12	10:00 p.m.

8

Administrators of the local school district must try to project student population growth for the next two years to help them determine staffing needs. To make reasonable estimates, they look up the total numbers of students in the district for a recent ten-year period and decide to organize the figures on a graph to show to the school board.

Data

2001 – 1,576
2002 – 1,680
2003 – 1,751
2004 – 1,607
2005 – 1,700
2006 – 1,848
2007 – 1,593
2008 – 1,445
2009 – 1,377
2010 – 1,210

line graph	circle graph	histogram	box-and-whisker plot
line graph	circle graph	histogram	box-and-whisker plot
line graph	circle graph	histogram	box-and-whisker plot
line graph	circle graph	histogram	box-and-whisker plot
line graph	circle graph	histogram	box-and-whisker plot
line graph	circle graph	histogram	box-and-whisker plot
line graph	circle graph	histogram	box-and-whisker plot
line graph	circle graph	histogram	box-and-whisker plot

Graphs and Statistics
EMC 3076
© Evan-Moor Corp.

Graphs and Statistics
EMC 3076
© Evan-Moor Corp.

Graphs and Statistics
EMC 3076
© Evan-Moor Corp.

Graphs and Statistics
EMC 3076
© Evan-Moor Corp.

Graphs and Statistics
EMC 3076
© Evan-Moor Corp.

Graphs and Statistics
EMC 3076
© Evan-Moor Corp.

Graphs and Statistics
EMC 3076
© Evan-Moor Corp.

Graphs and Statistics
EMC 3076
© Evan-Moor Corp.

Graphs and Statistics
EMC 3076
© Evan-Moor Corp.

Graphs and Statistics
EMC 3076
© Evan-Moor Corp.

Graphs and Statistics
EMC 3076
© Evan-Moor Corp.

Graphs and Statistics
EMC 3076
© Evan-Moor Corp.

Graphs and Statistics
EMC 3076
© Evan-Moor Corp.

Graphs and Statistics
EMC 3076
© Evan-Moor Corp.

Graphs and Statistics
EMC 3076
© Evan-Moor Corp.

Graphs and Statistics
EMC 3076
© Evan-Moor Corp.

Graphs and Statistics
EMC 3076
© Evan-Moor Corp.

Graphs and Statistics
EMC 3076
© Evan-Moor Corp.

Graphs and Statistics
EMC 3076
© Evan-Moor Corp.

Graphs and Statistics
EMC 3076
© Evan-Moor Corp.

Graphs and Statistics
EMC 3076
© Evan-Moor Corp.

Graphs and Statistics
EMC 3076
© Evan-Moor Corp.

Graphs and Statistics
EMC 3076
© Evan-Moor Corp.

Graphs and Statistics
EMC 3076
© Evan-Moor Corp.

Graphs and Statistics
EMC 3076
© Evan-Moor Corp.

Graphs and Statistics
EMC 3076
© Evan-Moor Corp.

Graphs and Statistics
EMC 3076
© Evan-Moor Corp.

Graphs and Statistics
EMC 3076
© Evan-Moor Corp.

Graphs and Statistics
EMC 3076
© Evan-Moor Corp.

Graphs and Statistics
EMC 3076
© Evan-Moor Corp.

Graphs and Statistics
EMC 3076
© Evan-Moor Corp.